C000088257

Connell Guide
to

———————

The Poetry
of
Robert Browning

———————

by
Jonathan Keates

Contents

NOTES

Introduction

Many of Robert Browning's poems are concerned with different aspects of human identity. In the great dramatic monologues, such as *Fra Lippo Lippi*, *Andrea del Sarto* and *My Last Duchess*, the question of exactly who is speaking obviously concerns us, but to what extent do the speaker's language and attitudes mirror those of the poet himself? In the various poems on the theme of love and sexual relationships which Browning included in his published collections *Dramatic Lyrics* and *Men and Women*, we inevitably want to know which of these spring directly from his personal experience. Even in an early work like the drama *Pippa Passes*, in which the poet's highly idiosyncratic verse style is heard for the first time, the issue of identity plays a key role in heightening dramatic tension.

Pippa, a poor girl apparently without parents or relatives, works as a silk-weaver in the north-Italian town of Asolo and has one day's holiday a year. Lacking money to enjoy herself properly, she decides to roam the streets, pausing occasionally outside the houses of various citizens to indulge her fantasy as to the lives they may be living there. These borrowed identities within her imagination set Pippa singing and the words of each song have a crucial, sometimes devastating impact on those who hear them. Ironically, her gift for intense empathy influences her own fate, when the final song touches the guilty conscience of the priest who, years earlier, fathered her with a local peasant woman.

Browning never felt a duty to reveal himself to the reader within his poetry. Though he admired several of the Romantic writers among the poetic generation immediately preceding his own, especially Shelley and Wordsworth, he was unwilling to follow their example by relating his discourse to the concept of a dominant ego, an "I" whose personal drama of feeling and experience formed the substance of a sustained narrative. Several of his works deliberately criticise the tendency, made fashionable by the Romantics, to see a poem as offering clues to its writer's identity and, by association, his private life. In 1874 Browning wrote two poems, *House* and *Shop*, which discuss this very question, challenging Wordsworth's claim, made on behalf of the sonnet form, that "With this same key/Shakespeare unlocked his heart".

As Browning sees it, the reader has no right to share an author's privacy:

"For a ticket, apply to the Publisher."
No: thanking the public, I must decline.
A peep through my window, if folk prefer;
But, please you, no foot over threshold of mine!

In *Shop* the tone is even more savagely one of "Keep your distance". The poet portrays himself as a shopkeeper with plenty of interesting merchandise on sale, but warns us against any temptation to identify what is shown in the window with the personal interests of the man or woman selling it:

Because a man has shop to mind
In time and place, since flesh must live,
Needs spirit lack all life behind,
All stray thoughts, fancies fugitive,
All loves except what trade can give?

The two poems seem at first to contradict each other, *House* denying the reader's right to investigate the author's private life, *Shop* rejecting the assumption that the artist lives purely within the confines of his art, with no alternative existence. Both emphasise the importance Browning clearly attached to separating his identity as an individual from his creative achievement as a poet.

So what was the man himself actually like? Perhaps appropriately, those who encountered Browning face to face had very different impressions. Thomas Carlyle, one of the Victorian era's great sages, critics and commentators, initially dismissed the young man as a dandy, fit for nothing better than "the turf and scamphood", but was soon won over by his "ingenuity, vivacity and Cockney gracefulness". Later the poet and essayist Walter Savage Landor, living in poverty as an expatriate in Florence, praised Browning's nobility of spirit in paying his rent for him. "Never was such generosity and such solicitude as this incomparable man has shown on my behalf."

Benjamin Jowett, Master of Balliol College, Oxford, told Florence Nightingale that "I had no idea that there was a perfectly sensible poet in the world, entirely free from vanity, jealousy or any other littleness & thinking no more of himself than if he were an ordinary man."

Others were not so enchanted. Tory prime minister Benjamin Disraeli dismissed Browning as "a noisy, conceited poet" after getting the worst of a

BROWNING'S MOST POPULAR POEMS?

Nowadays Robert Browning's most famous poem is *My Last Duchess*, admired for its sinister portrait of the menacing Duke of Ferrara. Certain other lyrics, such as *Meeting At Night, Evelyn Hope* and *A Toccata Of Galuppi's* find their way into verse collections, but Browning is altogether less of an anthology favourite than he used to be. Old-fashioned schoolroom poetry books, however, tell a different story. Fifty years ago the two poems most frequently included in the "everyone knows" category were *The Pied Piper Of Hamelin* and *How They Brought The Good News From Ghent To Aix*.

Both works, written within three years of each other, rely heavily on the poet's mastery of rhythm for their appeal. Each, what is more, turns aside from making any particularly profound statement on the vagaries of human behaviour, focusing instead on narrative and situation. One is a straightforward children's story in verse, the other interestingly consolidates on an earlier experiment in trying to simulate the sound discussion with him on the merits of various painters in the Royal Academy exhibition. Edmund Gosse, making a name for himself as a critic during the 1870s, was similarly put off at first by hearing "the loud trumpet-note" of Browning's conversation at a party, "already in full flood at a distance of twenty feet". Yet when the two eventually met privately, Gosse learned to cherish the poet's "image of intellectual vigour, armed at every point, but overflowing, none the less,

of galloping horse hooves.

The Pied Piper Of Hamelin, subtitled *A Child's Story,* was originally written to entertain young Willie Macready, son of Browning's friend the great tragic actor W. P. Macready. Willie was recovering from illness and Browning gave him the poem with the idea that when he'd finished reading it he might enjoy illustrating the story. Typically, the source of *The Pied Piper* lay in one of those obscure works only Robert Browning would ever trouble to read, a book by the Jacobean scholar Richard Verstegan called "Restitution Of Decayed Intelligence In Antiquities". Much concerned with the origin of ancient beliefs and customs, it features the story of a marvellous piper who freed the north-German city of Hameln, "Hamelin", from a plague of rats. Afterwards, having been refused his promised payment by the citizens, he carries off all their children, never to return.

Did this event actually happen, in "thirteen hundred and seventy six", as Browning tells us? Hameln itself dates it to 1284 and boasts a "Ratcatcher's House" to prove it. One of the theories behind the legend is that it derives from the ill-fated Children's Crusade of 1211, when thousands of German and Austrian with the geniality of strength".

The Victorian age saw the dawning of what would eventually become the modern cult of celebrity. Fans stalked their idols, begged for their autographs or photos and managed to obtain samples of their clothing and hair, even arming themselves with small pairs of scissors for the purpose. Whereas nowadays the quarry is a rock star or footballer, then it was politicians such as the Italian liberator Giuseppe

children set out for the Holy Land. Another relates it to choreomania, a mental disorder in which sufferers lose control of their limbs and seem to be perpetually dancing. Browning himself, towards the end of the poem, mentions a tradition among German-speaking communities in Transylvania (part of modern Romania) that they arrived there "out of some subterraneous prison/Into which they were trepanned/ Long ago in a mighty band/ Out of Hamelin town in Brunswick land."

Whatever the truth, the poet used his source material to create an enchanting fable, complete with the kind of moral conclusion Victorian parents and their children (sometimes less enthusiastically) expected to round off a nursery story. The fun element in *The Pied Piper* is offered by constantly shifting line-lengths and some of Browning's cheekiest rhyming, "havoc/ Vin-de-Grave, Hock", "pickle-tub-boards/ cupboards", "nuncheon/ luncheon/puncheon" and so on. Even the final couplet, underlining the importance of returning a favour done, has a neat twist in the rhyme:

"So Willie, let me and you be wipers
Out of scores with all men
- especially pipers!
And whether they pipe us *from* rats or *from* mice,
If we've promised them

Garibaldi or a leading personality in the world of the arts like the pianist-composer Franz Liszt or painter Lord Leighton. Writers were major objects of this new craze and several of them, Dickens and Thackeray included, took advantage of it to promote sales of their books.

Browning, too, was an inevitable target for celebrity hunters. By 1884 no less than 22 Browning Societies existed in Great Britain and the United

aught, let us keep our promise".

As for *How They Brought The Good News From Ghent To Aix* - Aix-la-Chapelle being the French name for the German town of Aachen – Browning owned up to being as mystified as anybody else by what exactly the good news in question might have been. The poem was written during his 1844 trip to Italy. "I was in a sailing vessel," he later recalled, "slowly making my way from Sicily to Naples in calm weather. I had a good horse at home in my stables and I thought to myself how much I should like a breezy gallop. As I could not ride on board ship, I determined to enjoy a ride in imagination."

The triple beat of speeding horse-hooves, first tried out in his poem *Through The Metidja To Abd-El-Kadr* (1842), made this an instant Browning favourite, though on a phonograph recording of the aged poet starting to recite it, we hear him give up after a few lines, exclaiming: "Oh, good God, I've gone and forgotten me own poetry!"

Perhaps both these poems will one day regain their popularity. Critics have little to say about them except as infallible proofs of Browning's dexterity as a maker of verses, but for pure enjoyment they have few rivals and as examples of poetry written first and foremost to be read aloud they are utterly perfect ■

States for the purpose of discussing his work and ideas. Though their activities were often ridiculed, these were a proof of the enormous respect in which he was held and of the way in which his poetry continued to fascinate contemporary readers through its extraordinary richness of ideas and the amazing comprehensiveness with which it distilled the variety of human experience.

But while the writer himself took care to keep his distance from what would now be called his fanbase, the question of what he was really like continued to intrigue his admirers. Among them was the American author Henry James, who had decided to settle in London for good following a series of visits to Europe during the 1870s. James was astonishingly perceptive and completely unruffled by the celebrities he encountered. They needed to meet his expectations and sometimes they failed: Tennyson, for instance, was "not Tennysonian enough" to satisfy Jamesian ideas of what the poet of *Maud* and *In Memoriam* ought to be, while the young Winston Churchill seemed so bumptious and self-absorbed that James felt positively admirable beside him. George Eliot, on the other hand, proved captivating enough, despite her lack of good looks, for the young American novelist to declare himself ready to fall in love with her.

Browning turned out to be more of a problem than any of these. James initially disliked the poet's vulgarity and "shrill interruptingness" when in

The Pied Piper of Hamelin, *Cecil Charles Windsor Aldin (1870-1935)*

company, "besides which, strange to say, his talk doesn't strike me as very good". Added to which, he was not particularly good at reading his own poems. "If you don't understand them, he understands them even less," noted James tartly. "He read them as if he hated them and would like to bite them to pieces."

Nevertheless the younger writer quickly grasped the truth that there were probably, in fact, several Brownings hidden beyond this disappointing face and compared this to a wall with a secret door. By pure coincidence the two of them ended up living in adjoining houses in De Vere Gardens, Kensington. James soon learned to value Browning's friendship and would compose a moving tribute to the poet, *Browning in Westminster Abbey*, following his funeral there on 31 December, 1889.

James's subtlest perspective on Browning is contained in his short story *The Private Life*, published in 1892. Here the whole issue of who Browning really was and the relationship between the artist and his identity are explored with genuine wit and sensitivity. The scene is a Swiss hotel under "a great bristling primeval glacier". Arriving here on holiday amid "undiminished snows and the fraternising tinkle of the unseen cattle", the anonymous narrator meets Lord and Lady Mellifont, Blanche Adney, a glamorous actress, her composer husband Vincent and "the great mature novelist" Clare Vawdrey, who she hopes will soon write her the perfect comedy to suit her talents. The question of whether Vawdrey will ever finish his play or is even actually at work on it is further complicated by ambiguous feelings towards him from the other members of the group.

There's a distinct sense that he doesn't live up to

their expectations as an author.

"He used to be called "subjective and introspective" in the weekly papers... He never talked about himself; and this was an article on which, though it would have been tremendously worthy of him, he apparently never even reflected. He had his hours and his habits, his tailor and his hatter, his hygiene and his particular wine, but all these things together never made up an attitude... He was exempt from variations, and not a shade either less or more nice in one place than in another. He differed from other people but never from himself... and he struck me as having neither moods nor sensibilities nor preferences... His opinions were sound and second-rate, and of his perceptions it was too mystifying to think."

Vawdrey – i.e.Browning – profoundly disappoints everybody by promising to recite one of his play's scenes from memory and promptly forgetting it all. James probably based this on the famous gramophone recording (made on a wax cylinder) in which Browning prepares to recite his poem *How They Brought The Good News From Ghent To Aix*, and is heard to stumble after a few lines (see p.9).

The story soon turns into a fascinating elaboration of the "Doppelganger" theme, in which two entirely disparate personalities inhabit a single individual, most famously illustrated in *Doctor Jekyll and Mr Hyde,* written by James's close friend Robert Louis Stevenson. In *The Private Life* the seemingly brilliant and charismatic Lord Mellifont (modelled on the painter Frederick Leighton) turns out to possess no kind of genuine identity whatever. Clare Vawdrey, on the other hand, has two wholly separate selves, public and private. While the first of these belongs to someone who "dines out and disappoints you" and "is always splendid, as your morning bath is splendid, or a sirloin of beef, or the railway service to Brighton", the latter remains intense, vital, sensitive but always careful to keep a distance from the banalities of social life. Thus Vawdrey uses his exterior self as a surrogate with which to protect his genius. "The world was vulgar and stupid, and the real man would have been a fool to come out for it, when he could gossip and dine by deputy."

If Henry James was accurate in his assessment – and as a friend and admirer of the poet he surely must have been – then Browning's work will tell us far more than his biographers ever could as to the real nature of the poet, his concerns and his obsessions.

Opposite: Michele Gordigiani's 1858 portrait of Browning. The portrait was commissioned by an American admirer of Browning, Sophie Eckley, when he was living with his wife in Florence. She felt the likeness an "Incomparable Portrait by far the best ever taken", though the critic W.M. Rossetti commented that the face was "treated with too much morbidezza, so as to lack some of that extreme keenness, which characterised Browning".

AT A GLANCE: TEN OF BROWNING'S GREATEST POEMS

MY LAST DUCHESS

Most famous of all Browning's dramatic monologues, *My Last Duchess*, written in 1842, is also one of his earliest essays in the genre. The speaker is a Renaissance Duke of Ferrara, preparing to wed the daughter of a count, whose envoy is arranging final marriage settlements. The duke shows him a portrait of his last duchess, kept behind a curtain, and nonchalantly hints that she has been put to death for being too free with her favours and smiles. A closing reference to a bronze statue of Neptune suggests that the murdered duchess, like her picture, is of no greater value to her husband than his art collection.

PORPHYRIA'S LOVER

Another sinister monologue with a focus on a murdered woman. The speaker has killed his mistress Porphyria at a crucial moment when her beauty achieved a particular radiance, which he wants to preserve as exclusively his own. Is he mad? Almost certainly, yet it is the lucidity with which he describes the whole episode which lends the poem its uniquely gruesome impact. Dated 1836, this was one of the first of Browning's shorter works to be published.

THE BISHOP ORDERS HIS TOMB AT SAINT PRAXED'S CHURCH

Originally published in *Hood's Magazine* in 1845, this poem has always been admired for the way in which Browning skilfully sums up the worldliness and sensuality of the Italian Renaissance, using a seemingly venerable

Catholic bishop as his mouthpiece. The old cleric in fact has nothing spiritual about him. Round his deathbed prowl his bastard sons, whom he orders to prepare an expensive tomb for him inside one of Rome's oldest churches, largely as a final gesture of defiance towards his lifelong rival, also buried there. By the end of the poem the dying bishop realises that his family has no intention of honouring his wishes, heirs as they all are to his greed and ruthlessness.

LOVE AMONG THE RUINS

This was the opening item in Browning's most highly-regarded collection of poems, *Men And Women*, published in 1855 and dedicated to his wife Elizabeth Barrett, herself a distinguished poet. Its setting is the open country around Rome, which he had explored on recent visits to the city. The Campagna, as this area was known, mixed pastures and farms with an impressive scatter of ruined buildings from Roman antiquity, including bridges, aqueducts and tombs. Browning uses these as images of human impermanence, contrasted with the enduring love of the woman he addresses.

UP AT A VILLA – DOWN IN THE CITY

The voice assumed by the poet here is that of "an Italian person of quality", a cash-strapped Tuscan nobleman forced to spend more time than he would like at his rustic villa instead of living in town. Browning pokes indulgent fun at the Italian dislike of the countryside (implicitly contrasted with the sort of pastoral nostalgia his English readers are likely to feel) while using a wealth of small details to evoke the vitality and colour of the urban scene in nineteenth-century Italy.

FRA LIPPO LIPPI

Through the mouth of the Renaissance painter Filippo Lippi Browning expresses aspects of his own artistic credo. Brought up in a Carmelite monastery, where he has unwillingly become a friar, Lippo enjoys the nightlife of the Florentine streets. Arrested by a posse of watchmen, he tells them his story. At its centre is a justification of himself as an artist dealing with reality rather than purveying an ideal world. Lippo's sacred art uses everyday observation and models drawn from life to emphasize God's presence on earth and the divine gift of "simple beauty".

A TOCCATA OF GALUPPI'S

Several of Browning's poems are set in Venice – the city where he died in 1889 – and this is the best of these, a haunting evocation of the once-great maritime metropolis in the 18th century, when it had become a place of decadence, idleness and vanity. To help him conjure up the imagined atmosphere, he summons the ghost of Baldassare Galuppi, a multi-talented composer of the period, noted, among other things, for his keyboard sonatas. Galuppi here becomes both a witness to Venetian decay and a prophet of human mortality. Browning passionately loved music, but this poem, one of his simplest in terms of form and expression, explores a great deal more than the poet's personal enthusiasm.

CHILDE ROLAND TO THE DARK TOWER CAME

The title is taken from a snatch of a ballad quoted by the Fool in Shakespeare's *King Lear*. Browning always spoke of this poem, first published in *Men And Women*, as essentially "a kind of dream" and stated that he had no idea of its true meaning. A number of elements from fairy tales, legends, medieval art and Italian landscape combine to create a world of symbol and fantasy which continues to challenge the ingenuity of scholars, critics and ordinary readers.

ANDREA DEL SARTO

The painter Andrea del Sarto (1486 - 1531) was greatly admired in his own day for the flawless finish and perfection of his work. By the time this poem was written in 1855, however, he had come to seem a somewhat cold and lifeless technician. Here Browning imagines him as inherently a successful failure, a figure corrupted by his own facility with the brush, preyed upon by envy of other artists (including Raphael and Michelangelo) and powerless to control his grasping, manipulative wife, openly conducting an affair with a man she calls "the cousin". The whole poem can be viewed as a companion piece to *Fra Lippo Lippi*, negative and dark-hued where the other is bursting with triumphant affirmation.

YOUTH AND ART

For many Browning readers this poem comes as a complete surprise. Set in the bohemian world of his Victorian artistic contemporaries, it portrays two young people, a sculptor and a singer, dedicated to becoming the best in their chosen fields. He is successful, she less so, but each in their different ways has carved out a position in society. The point is that the pair of them missed out on the one thing which might have given them true happiness and fulfilment, a love affair with each other. The wit, irony and use of sexual symbolism in the poem make it one of Browning's most piquant enunciations of the belief, expressed elsewhere in his work, that the ideal moment is there for the taking and should never be let go.

What did Browning believe in?

In his own lifetime Browning was hailed by many of his readers as a sage, a guru, a wise man communicating a distinctive philosophy. This assumption that the poet had something to tell them beyond the immediate circumstances forming the background to a particular poem and the experience it distils was characteristic of a specifically Victorian attitude to creativity, one which required moral uplift and a distinctive ethical message from an artist's work. Reading the age's leading novelists, figures such as George Eliot, Dickens, Trollope or Mrs Gaskell, we become used to the presence of an overriding morality by which the various characters are tested. This impulse was not confined solely to literature. Paintings like William Holman Hunt's *The Awakening of Conscience* or the various treatments of the Arthurian legend by Edward Burne- Jones make an obvious bid for a resonance beyond the purely narrative or decorative.

In 1905, about 30 years after Browning's death, the essayist, novelist and critic G.K. Chesterton, in his study of the poet, made one of the most successful attempts at summing up what, to various readers, seemed one of the more baffling questions about someone who had always been thought of as a "difficult" writer. What exactly did Robert Browning, man and artist, believe in and how were his beliefs reflected in his poetry? The essence of the poet's creed, according to Chesterton, was "the hope which lies in the imperfection of man". Browning saw that incompleteness in human beings was far more interesting than perfection for the way in which it seemed to open up a path to immortality. As long as there was something missing, the individual could look forward to becoming immortal. A life where perfection had not yet been achieved, where some sort of flaw or personality defect existed, was by its very nature more promising than one whose potential had been satisfactorily fulfilled.

This contrast is made abundantly clear for us if we place two of the poet's finest dramatic monologues side by side. One of these is *Fra Lippo Lippi*, the other *Andrea del Sarto*, and the speaker in each is a well-known Italian Renaissance painter. In the former poem, Filippo Lippi, a Florentine artist, speaks frankly as to his life and character, neither of them particularly admirable – he is a friar of the Carmelite order who repeatedly breaks his vow of chastity – and proclaims his abundant joy in the creative process underlying his paintings. Browning was doubtless well aware that all of Lippi's surviving works are religious in their subject matter, but the poem seeks to underline an essential earthiness beneath their spirituality.

As presented to us here, Lippo Lippi has been seen by some readers as positively evil, but this is to miss the point. Browning's aim in presenting him as a low-life character is to show how our spiritual impulses, our yearning for higher things and for the presence of God on earth, can be stimulated by the talent and inventiveness of an inherently worldly human being, someone who hangs out with prostitutes and petty criminals in the dark back streets of Renaissance Florence. One of the issues at the heart of the poem concerns our expectation that the quality of an artist's private life should somehow reflect the profundity and seriousness we are accustomed to look for within his work. The truth, as Browning realises, is that however much we may want artists as individuals to match the inspiration offered by their art, we have no right to demand this of them. Thus he deliberately sets out to challenge one of Victorian culture's most cherished ideals and to prove that human nature, being what it is, this can never be adequately realised.

In the process, Lippo Lippi becomes the spokesman both for a more realistic approach to the relationship between art and life and, by association, for those notions of "art for art's sake" which painters, poets and aesthetic theorists of the late 19th century, with Oscar Wilde as their spokesman, would eventually make popular. Lippi explicitly rejects the instructions given him by the prior of his monastery and the senior clergy to

Make them forget there's such a thing as flesh.
Your business is to paint the souls of men...

Paint the soul, never mind the legs and arms.

That, Lippi implies, is just the point. Painting souls, he argues, is impossible unless you can capture the essence of the physical body first of all. In a striking echo of John Keats's dictum

Beauty is truth, truth beauty: that is all
Ye know on earth and all ye need to know"

the artist states his credo:

If you get simply beauty and nought else,
You get about the best thing God invents.

Lippo links this directly to his own angry yearning for the secular world, which drives him to slip out of the cloister from time to time into the Florentine streets:

A laugh, a cry, the business of the world...
And my whole soul revolves, the cup runs over,
The world and life's too big to pass for a dream,
And I do these wild things in sheer despite.

Browning's masterstroke in this astonishingly bold, confident essay in using a vividly realised historical figure to project a view of the purpose and function of art, is to interweave Lippi's monologue with snatches of an erotic ballad heard drifting down the street as he is speaking. Smutty, loquacious and completely fearless as he pours out his mixture of autobiography and personal philosophy to the listening watchmen detaining him during a night patrol – the irony here is that they are unlikely to appreciate much of what Lippi tells them – he is one of the most engaging figures in Browning's busy and varied portrait gallery.

Andrea del Sarto is Lippo Lippi's melancholy opposite. The poem bearing his name is subtitled *Called "The Faultless Painter"*, which immediately lends it an air of ambiguity, since our inevitable question must be whether faultless equals perfect or whether we require an artist to be faultless in the first place. Browning clearly doesn't. Where he is concerned, painters, writers or musicians are

BROWNING'S BOOKS

What has always amazed – and not infrequently deterred – those making their first acquaintance with Browning is the sheer depth of his reading. How much are we ourselves expected to have read before we can understand him properly? Is he merely showing off, with his references to minor Italian Baroque painters, 17th-century Breton pirates, Provençal troubadours and long-forgotten Regency sex scandals? John Pettigrew, a recent modern editor of the collected poems, tells us that "the ideal Browning annotator needs – besides sympathy – to be thoroughly at home with music, art, and seven or eight languages and literatures, to know the Bible and the plays of Euripides and Aristophanes (and Victorian scholarship not guaranteed respect simply for their technical perfection. The very fact that his paintings were considered to be without fault damns Andrea from the outset. He is in any case seriously flawed as an individual. At the beginning of the poem he has returned from France, where King Francis I, "that humane great monarch", had invited him to work in the royal chateau at Fontainebleau. It is made clear that the artist has failed to honour his contract with the king, while accepting a salary which he has used to build himself a house in Florence:

I took his coin, was tempted and complied,
And built this house and sinned, and all is said.

on them) by heart, to be intimately familiar – for a start – with Keats and Shelley and Donne and Milton and Homer... and the *Illustrated London News* and Johnson's *Dictionary*... and to have read all those strange books, which, one comes to believe, have had in their long history only one reader – Robert Browning".

Dismissing all this as "pretentiousness" on Browning's part is simply a convenient excuse for ducking one of the principal challenges offered to us by his work. He wants to share with his own readers the excitement of the worlds he has been busy exploring within the vast universe of the printed word. More significantly, he is eager to show how exciting ordinary experience can be by placing it in as wide a range of different cultural contexts as possible. He uses what he has read as a medium through which to filter his humane perception of the world at its best and worst ■

The simple style Browning uses in *Andrea del Sarto*, very different from the notoriously mannered idiom characterising many of his other poems, is clearly deliberate. It implies that the speaker has no defence, having reached the limit of his resources, and its impact on us seems to invite a sort of sneaking pity for someone who, whether as artist or man, simply lacks the greatness of soul to rise to the challenges offered by his immense painterly proficiency.

Central to this portrait of human weakness is Andrea's obsession with his worthless mistress Lucrezia, a gold-digger currently carrying on an affair with a man referred to as "the Cousin", whose gambling debts she has got Andrea to pay. The painter himself, we gather, is at work on a fresco sequence and a portrait for another of Lucrezia's admirers, purely so as to "get you thirteen scudi for the ruff". These men hanging around her possess a certain skill which Andrea, for all his money and expertise, cannot hope to acquire. "Ah, but what does he,/The Cousin! what does he to please you more?" The obtuseness of this question tells us everything about the speaker's inadequacy.

Both professionally and personally Andrea knows himself to be a failure. There's a bogus bravado, as well as a good deal of vulgarity, in the way he sums up his career:

My father and my mother died of want...
They were born poor, lived poor, and poor they died:

And I have laboured somewhat in my time
And not been paid profusely. Some good son
Paint my two hundred pictures – let him try!

Andrea, as we have already guessed, will not have
sons. The younger generation is represented for him
by his rivals Raphael and Michelangelo. He knows
that

There burns a truer light of God in them,
In their vexed beating stuffed and stopped-up brain
Heart, or whate'er else, than goes on to prompt
This low-pulsed forthright craftsman's hand of mine.

The critic and literary historian Leonée Ormond,
in an essay on "Browning and Painting", has pointed
out that *Fra Lippo Lippi* and *Andrea del Sarto* are less
concerned specifically with their subjects' works than
with the individual artist's life and personality, based
on hints from Giorgio Vasari's Renaissance classic,
The Lives of the Most Noble Painters and Sculptors.
She goes on to say that "each of these poems is
about the craft of poetry and about Browning as a
practitioner".

Such a worthwhile observation does not, of
course, invalidate Chesterton's point as to the poet's
philosophy being based to a significant extent on "the
hope which lies in the imperfection of man". The
two monologues quoted here represent alternate
facets of this idea. While there is no hope for Andrea,

whatever his complete grasp of technique, Fra Lippo Lippi has a confident mastery which transcends the directionless hedonism of his bohemian lifestyle. In discussing these and other monologues Chesterton is categorical on the important issue of whether or not Browning is holding his speakers up to ridicule. "They are not satires or attacks upon their subjects," he declares, "they are not even harsh and unfeeling exposures of them. They are defences; they say or are intended to say the best that can be said for the persons with whom they deal." The point about even the most contemptible or frightening of these figures, the greedy, emphatically unspiritual prelate in *The Bishop Orders His Tomb At Saint Praxed's Church*, for example, or the sinister Duke of Ferrara in *My Last Duchess*, is that "they are real somewhere, and may at any given moment begin to speak poetry... Every one of these meagre swindlers, while admitting a failure in all things relative, claims an awful alliance with the Absolute."

This kind of humanity in the poet transcends our traditional view of the Victorians as censorious, unforgiving and hidebound in their moral expectations as to one another's conduct. But was Browning really a Christian and was this indulgent stance of his the product of his upbringing? A family friend described his father as "a serene, untroubled soul, conscious of no moral or theological problem to disturb his serenity, and as gentle as a gentle woman". Both parents, according to Browning, had "a childlike faith in goodness", which he inherited only up to a point. Personal experience tended to make him rather more sceptical as to people's intentions, especially those of political figures or those who basked too readily in their own celebrity – something which, to his credit, the world-famous poet never chose to do.

Browning's engagement with Christianity forms a continuous thread linking early, middle and late poems, hence giving us the sense of a spiritual journey in its various stages, but one which doesn't anticipate or indeed demand completion. He never experienced a serious moment of doubt in a fashion we might expect of a Victorian writer confronted by what his contemporary Matthew Arnold defined as "the fierce intellectual life of our century". In his first major poem, *Pauline*, published in 1833, he implicitly rejects the atheism of his boyhood's literary hero Percy Bysshe Shelley, affirming instead the importance of "a need, a trust, a yearning after God". Such hankerings for something to believe in is fundamental to our understanding of Browning's ethos throughout his poetry. Several key works of his maturity dwell on the concept of Christ as an incarnate human being, living and dying in the world and presenting mankind with a practical role model. As he says in *Pauline:*

Oft have I stood by thee,
Have I been keeping lonely watch with thee

In the damp night by weeping Olivet,
Or leaning on thy bosom, proudly less,
Or dying with thee on the lonely cross,
Or witnessing thine outburst from the tomb.

It was Browning's wife, Elizabeth Barrett, herself a hugely esteemed poet with a reputation established well before her husband's, who perceptively remarked of him that "it is his way to *see* things as passionately as other people *feel* them". This idea of witness as being vital to spiritual experience was perhaps part of the inheritance from his evangelical parents (his mother was a devout Congregationalist) but it continued to play an essential role in the imaginative world of religion, metaphysics and philosophy shaped by his verse. There are undoubtedly several moments where Browning, whatever his horror of self-disclosure, seems actually to be recording a personal epiphany or revelation.

One such comes in *Bishop Blougram's Apology*, from the collection *Men And Women*, a poem whose background is the mid-19th-century ferment created by the revival of English Roman Catholicism, drawing converts among Anglicans disenchanted with the sober evangelicalism of the established Church of England. The figure of the eponymous Bishop Blougram was suggested by Henry Wiseman, Archbishop of Westminster, whom Pope Pius IX had made the first English cardinal since the

ROBERT BROWNING, D.C.L.,

THE RING AND BOOK-MAKER FROM RED COTTON NIGHT-CAP COUNTRY.

Cartoon of Browning by Edward Linley Sambourne in Punch, 1882

Reformation. Browning acknowledged the likeness. "Certainly I intended it for Cardinal Wiseman, but I don't consider it a satire, there is nothing hostile in it." The portrait, superficially at least, is scarcely flattering. Blougram is a snob – a certain kind of

English Catholic, especially a convert like the 20th-century novelist Evelyn Waugh, has always delighted in his church's historic links with titled nobility and "old families" – and he is also a consummate performer, versatile, not to say devastating, in argument, but evidently lacking in the Christian virtues of charity and compassion. His "apology" (Browning uses the term in its original Greek sense, which involves the speaker or writer setting out a case for himself) wipes the floor with the journalist Mr Gigadibs, a youthful sceptic in religious matters who has clearly been hoping to score points off the hypocritical, pleasure-loving Catholic prelate.

Yet through the mouth of someone with whom, theoretically, the poet has no genuine common ground, Browning develops a complex sequence of arguments in defence of religious faith and emphasising the inherent sterility of doubt. Morality, Bishop Blougram suggests, is pointless without a set of principles to underpin it. If doubt has any purpose, it is that of strengthening belief.

> *You call for faith:*
> *I show you doubt, to prove that faith exists.*
> *The more of doubt, the stronger faith, I say,*
> *If faith o'ercomes doubt.*

Bishop Blougram's Apology covers a fascinatingly wide range of cultural and political reference, illustrating the poet's dizzying alertness to the contemporary European civilization surrounding him. There are allusions to the highly controversial German intellectuals David Strauss and Ludwig Feuerbach, both of whom were attacked for trying to demystify Christianity by placing it in a rational historical context. There are glances at the Italian Risorgimento and its impact on the increasingly entrenched position of the papacy (in the persons of Pius IX and his chief adviser Cardinal Antonelli) as a last bastion of conservative reaction in a world of secular empiricism. There is an amusing vignette, by Browning the music-lover, of the composer Giuseppe Verdi, with "his orchestra of salt-box, tongs and bones", deferring, "through all the roaring and the wreaths", to the genius of the elderly Gioacchino Rossini, doyen of Italian operatic masters.

What this all adds up to is encapsulated in a passage early in the poem, when Blougram, having lulled Gigadibs into believing that not much separates them from one another in terms of their essential cynicism, invokes as a counterweight the dramatic effects of a suddenly reawakened spirituality on the human soul.

Just when we are safest, there's a sunset touch,
A fancy from a flower-bell, some one's death,
A chorus-ending from Euripides,
And that's enough for fifty hopes and fears
As old and new at once as nature's self,
To rap and knock and enter in our soul,

Take hands and dance there, a fantastic ring,
Round the ancient idol, on his base again,
The grand Perhaps!

These lines from *Bishop Blougram's Apology* are some of Browning's best known, and that final "grand Perhaps" has been invoked as a means of placing him within a specific context of Victorian religious doubt. A poet who seems close to him in this respect is one whom he powerfully influenced, Thomas Hardy, among the most original poetic voices of the late 19th and early 20th centuries. Hardy's poem *The Oxen*, though actually written in 1915, directly inherits this idea of the divine impulse as something human beings eternally long for. In childhood, Hardy tells us, it was easy for him to share the country superstition that at midnight on Christmas Eve the farm animals knelt in reverence to mark the birth of Christ. For adults, however, such faith is more problematic

So fair a fancy few would weave
In these years! Yet, I feel,
If someone said on Christmas Eve,
"Come, see the oxen kneel
In the lonely barton by yonder comb
Our childhood used to know"
I should go with him in the gloom,
Hoping it might be so.

The difference between Browning and Hardy lies in the ways whereby the former's version of "Hoping it might be so" leans far more heavily towards an idea that in the case of Jesus Christ it genuinely was so. Several of Browning's most important poems, such as *An Epistle of Karshish the Physician* and *A Death in the Desert*, are based on the idea of an intelligent, thoughtful non-Christian confronting either the historical Christ or one of his disciples and being clearly unsettled or else genuinely moved by the experience. Sometimes this reaction takes the form of excited curiosity, sometimes, on the other hand, the speaker's determined scepticism is tinged with fear and defensiveness.

Donald Thomas, in his biographical study *Robert Browning: A Life With Life* (1982), makes the point, with reference to *Men And Women*, that the poet "repeatedly returns to attack the fallacy that doubt or unbelief was either more honest or more intellectually productive than religious faith". This approach is skilfully exploited in *Cleon*, a monologue which seems partly to have been inspired by Matthew Arnold's verse drama *Empedocles on Etna*, published in 1852. Cleon himself is a Greek poet of the first century AD, living and writing at a time when Hellenic culture, though still an indicator of sophistication in the Roman empire, was beginning a gradual decline. As always, the poem imagines another person being addressed, in this case a king named Protus. Browning, well-versed in classical

Greek, actually uses the ancient term "tyrant" for him, meaning "absolute ruler" but without the pejorative significance such a word possesses nowadays.

Protus, we learn, has been building a tower for himself, and in doing so has been led to ponder the likelihood of an afterlife and the whole issue of immortality. Cleon's response to these speculations seems designed to alienate the reader. To start with,

VICTORIAN FAITH AND DOUBT

One of the most important aspects of the century in which Browning lived was its role as a vast battleground between Christianity, in various denominations, and its supposed enemies represented by science, education and technology, with their challenges to traditional religious dogma. During the 1840s, geologists led the charge, by proving that the earth was far older than previously reckoned. This attack on the very roots of the biblical creation story was given its most drastic impetus with the publication of Charles Darwin's *The Origin of Species* (1859), setting out the principles of evolution in the natural world.

Meanwhile, the textual authenticity of the Bible itself was being critically examined by a leading Anglican cleric, Bishop John William Colenso, amid fierce attacks from the church establishment. Anglicanism in any case saw its position in British national life threatened by the growing popularity of Nonconformist churches.

he dwells on the brilliance – or at least the overall virtuosity – of his achievement as a poet, able to turn out anything from "an epos on thy hundred plates of gold" to

> *the little chant*
> *So sure to rise from every fishing-bark*
> *When, lights at prow, the seamen haul their net.*

Its clergy had to come to terms with the effects both of American-style Protestant evangelism and of a newly energised Roman Catholic church vigorously recruiting converts among the most powerful echelons of Victorian society.

Atheism, agnosticism or religious doubts openly expressed were serious matters in the England of Robert Browning, and we need to appreciate their significance as we read him and his contemporaries. The reality of a wavering faith in the aftermath of personal loss underlies Alfred Tennyson's *In Memoriam*, an extended lyric sequence designed as a record of inner turmoil following the death of a close friend. Elsewhere Matthew Arnold, noted as one of the most incisive prose commentators on the mood and temper of the Victorian age, uses poems such as *Dover Beach*, *The Scholar Gypsy* and *Stanzas From The Grande Chartreuse* to examine the anguished confusion surrounding the whole issue of religious belief and the resulting problems of engaging with the complexities of modern life. Poetic statements of this kind repay reading alongside Browning poems such as *Christmas Eve And Easter Day* or *Rabbi Ben Ezra* for the different ways in which they reflect on what, for many Victorians, was one of the era's major issues ∎

In addition, Cleon is a philosopher, who has written three books on the soul, a painter, architect and musical theorist. "In brief, all arts are mine," he smugly declares. His absorption with art and his life of creative enterprise cannot shield him, on the other hand, from the simple truth that art is no substitute for the direct experience of reality. Knowledge, expertise and understanding are counterbalanced by sensual impulse and simple emotion:

> *Indeed, to know is something, and to prove*
> *How all this beauty might be enjoyed, is more:*
> *But, knowing nought, to enjoy is something too.*

Will Cleon's works survive? Can a life of straining after absolute perfection ensure him immortality? What terrifies him is the plain fact that nothing can hold back old age, that even as insight grows sharper, the body is decaying. He dreads

> *The consummation coming past escape*
> *When I shall know most, and yet least enjoy.*

As so often in Browning's poetry, the importance of enjoyment for its own sake is vital to the argument here. To ensure the survival of this sensation, Cleon finds himself longing for the one element his Greek pagan culture has denied him, the existence of an afterlife in which "I, the feeling, thinking, acting man" will somehow manage to cheat death.

At the monologue's close, with Cleon's mask
of complacency starting to crack beneath his
increasingly fretful musing on the value of art as
a guarantee that its creator's spirit will endure for
ever, Browning slyly inserts a postscript as the multi-
talented man of genius signs off his letter to the
tyrant – evidently a humbler and more worthwhile
human being than he himself is. We are told that
Protus, curious as to the possibility of a life beyond
the grave, is in correspondence with "one called
Paulus" on the subject. This is none other than
Paul of Tarsus, the Christian apostle, and the Greek
is shocked that somebody of this kind, "a mere
barbarian Jew", should have access to knowledge
inaccessible to philosophers like himself. As for the
Christians he represents, "their doctrine could be
held by no sane man". This neatly ironic conclusion
leaves us feeling pity for Cleon, with all his
intellectual smugness, the same sort of pity, indeed,
that we feel for Andrea del Sarto, equally bereft of
any consolation likely to be offered by the possession
of outstanding artistic talents. The implication is that
Cleon's scorn for Saint Paul's message essentially
damns him, Browning having grasped the truth that
all cultures suffer from too great a sense of their own
self-sufficiency. Christianity, with its promise of
future salvation, will ultimately destroy, or at least
render obsolete, most of the values Cleon stands for.

Ultimately, Browning's credo is summed up for us
in a single line from a poem he published in 1864,

James Lee's Wife, a sequence of lyrics portraying the breakdown of a marriage and making use of material dating back almost 30 years to the period of *Pippa Passes*. In a section entitled "Among The Rocks" the encouragement to "Give earth yourself, go up for gain above!" expresses the poet's philosophy in a nutshell. A total engagement with the business of living, whether through indulging the senses or through the acquisition of varied experience in as many varied forms as possible, need not invalidate a spiritual dimension. The intensely "grounded" worldliness of Browning's characters offers them an ideal medium in which to gain heightened consciousness of a spiritual dimension.

How Victorian was Browning?

Central to Browning's idea of the links between the inner life and earthly experience is a sense of what he calls "the good minute". The phrase comes from one of his most memorable love poems, *Two In The Campagna*, written while he was living in Rome during the 1850s. Its dozen stanzas portray a situation in which a lover's upsurge of passion is darkened by a feeling that the woman he loves is, in the end, not quite interesting enough and

Robert Browning *by Eveleen W.H. Myers c.1889-1891*

that their relationship is essentially an ephemeral one. The image of the pair wandering through the beautiful countryside beyond the walls of Rome, its fields scattered with ancient tombs from the days of the Caesars, becomes subtly de-romanticised by Browning's use of symbols derived from the plant and insect life of the late spring landscape surrounding the two lovers. Anybody reading the poem will immediately catch the implication of intense sexual bonding created by lines like:

Such life here, through such lengths of hours,
Such miracles performed in play,
Such primal naked forms of flowers,
Such letting nature have her way
While heaven looks from its towers!

The speaker, prompted by the entrancing fecundity of the landscape around him, seems to be on the verge of inviting his mistress to consummate their affair through a physical act of sex. Almost at once, however, he realises that she does not mean enough to him as a lover for this to matter. Nevertheless he kisses her and then

I pluck the rose
And love it more than tongue can speak –
Then the good minute goes.

This concept of the good minute, a crucial moment

of perfect sexual fulfillment between man and woman, is a continuing theme of Browning's poetry from *Pauline* right through to *Asolando*. Sometimes, as in *The Statue And The Bust*, he takes the idea still further, shaping a whole philosophy, within a single poem, around the importance to us of seizing our opportunities when we can, rather than allowing ourselves to be unduly influenced by social convention, ethical scruples or pure prejudice. Probably written in 1855, the poem is based on the scandalous liaison between the Florentine Grand Duke Ferdinando de' Medici (1549 – 1608) and Bianca Capello, who had eloped from her native Venice to Florence with a bank clerk she had secretly married. Ferdinando, having put his first wife to death, had Bianca's husband murdered and was then free to wed her, but their marriage proved unhappy and the duke's brother Francesco, impatient to seize power, disposed of the pair with the help of a poisoned apple tart.

In *The Statue And The Bust,* Browning completely re-shapes this story for his own purposes, taking as his starting point the fact that Ferdinando first caught sight of Bianca while riding past her window. In this new version there is no marriage, let alone a toxic apple tart, as the two lovers fail to bring their affair to a successful climax. Instead they are left separately contemplating what might have happened if only each had seized the chance offered them at the critical moment. To console herself,

Bianca has her sculptured head and shoulders – the bust of the poem's title – placed outside her window and Ferdinand commissions an equestrian statue of himself looking up at her, to be set up in the square below. Art thus perpetuates the unfulfilled promise implied by their initial encounter. Browning draws the moral as follows:

If you choose to play! – is my principle.
Let a man contend to the uttermost
For his life's set prize, be what it will!

The American critic George Santayana, in his essay "The Poetry of Barbarism" (1900), condemned Browning for believing that " the exercise of energy is the absolute good, irrespective of motives or of consequences", but as Philip Drew, in *Browning and Philosophy* (1974), points out, this doesn't necessarily mean that Browning thinks one set of motives to be as good as another.

We are back once again with the question of how much the poet's personal value system is mirrored in his work. Such issues of sincerity and integrity were of major significance to the men and women of Browning's own time. The word "truth" and all that it represented arguably mattered far more to the Victorians than it does to us. It turns up frequently of a whole variety of different works produced during this period – the radical newspaper *Truth*, for example, Julius and Francis Hare's popular theological essays *Guesses At Truth*, or W.S. Gilbert's "fairy comedy" *The Palace Of Truth*. No wonder Oscar Wilde, that witty saboteur of Victorian received wisdom (and an admirer of Browning) was so eager to stand the whole notion of truth on its head and poke fun at it.

So just how Victorian, according to our traditional view of his age, was Robert Browning? A good deal less so, from many aspects, than his most distinguished poetic contemporary Alfred Tennyson, regarded as a kind of spiritual guru by Queen Victoria herself. He had, after all, outraged Victorian convention through his secret marriage to Elizabeth Moulton-Barrett in 1846. This, and their subsequent elopement to Italy, alienated Elizabeth permanently from several members of her family and earned severe criticism from various of her friends.

The fact that they were hardly a brace of giddy young lovers – Browning was 34 and Elizabeth 40 – seems to have had no bearing on such disapproval. By living abroad in Catholic Italy, what is more, the Brownings automatically courted censure from Victorian England, predominantly Protestant and regarding Italians as frivolous, immoral and given to unsavoury habits. Had not the great naval hero Lord Nelson once dismissed Italy as "a country of fiddlers and poets, whores and scoundrels"? Annual visits by Robert and Elizabeth to France during the 1850s scarcely improved the picture, since the Victorians saw French society as thoroughly decadent and Paris itself as a modern Babylon, stewing in depravity.

Browning has often been seen at his least
Victorian in the treatment of sex in his poems. An
extraordinary empathy with women, a fondness for
their company and the continuing presence of valued
female friends throughout his life enabled him to
write imaginatively from a woman's point of view
and to acknowledge, in the face of contemporary
mores and decorum, the imperatives of female
sexuality. How difficult a subject was an individual's
erotic life for him to approach in the context of his
19th-century readership, as a respected voice among
the poets of the age?

For the past 100 years, or at least since the
publication of Lytton Strachey's iconoclastic
Eminent Victorians in 1918, we have tended to view
Browning's age as one of ferocious repression,
in which every kind of natural human impulse –
emotional, physical, sexual – was stifled under a pall
of humourlessness, obsessive reticence and flagrant
hypocrisy. The urban myth that Victorians draped
the legs of their grand pianos with embroidered
cloth covers because their apparent nakedness was
potentially suggestive continues to enjoy a robust
currency. Notions of this kind, many of them without

Opposite: William Powell Frith's A Private View at the Royal Academy, *1881.
Browning, bare-headed and with a white beard, stands talking to an unknown woman
in a green dress. Frith painted the picture after the death of Disraeli, opposing his
historical achievments and the ephemeral Aesthetic movement, personified in the
figure of Oscar Wilde (behind the boy in the green suit). Other figures include the
novelist Anthony Trollope, Prime Minister William Gladstone and actress Ellen Terry.*

any foundation in fact, encourage the belief that certain areas of human activity were forever off-limits to Victorian writers, most of all in the field of sexual relationships.

In fact Victorian literature, especially poetry, is widely concerned with erotic experience. The critic Isobel Armstrong, in an essay on "Browning and Victorian Poetry of Sexual Love", explains this as follows:

> The sensible view is that sexual love is a subject simply *because* overt reference was so difficult. The need to write about experiences which were so hedged round with confusions and fears must have been immense.

Several of the most famous poems by Browning's contemporaries stand out precisely for the skill with which their authors have handled such potentially hazardous subject matter. Tennyson's *Mariana,* for example, explicitly devises a web of symbolism to convey its themes of thwarted desire and sexual frustration, while his *Lady Of Shalott* blatantly eroticises the figure of Sir Lancelot as a spur to its heroine to forsake her world of creative seclusion amid mirrors and shadows. Christina Rossetti's *Goblin Market* shapes a whole world of temptation from the sensual excitement created by the fruits offered to the all-too susceptible Laura by the sinister goblin pedlars.

The problem for poets in a world which laid so much stress on decency, propriety and the question of what could or couldn't be discussed was to find ways of articulating sexual and erotic experience without laying themselves open to charges of obscenity or offending their more sensitive readers. Browning clearly enjoyed such a challenge and his work is rich in poems which explicitly acknowledge love as a physical as well as an emotional impulse. This concept of the "good minute" entails a shared perception of this reality by the two lovers in their surrender to passion.

At its simplest, this idea controls *Meeting At Night*, one of the finest short poems in the language. Evoked here is the image of a man landing his boat on a beach, crossing some fields and arriving at his lover's house. He taps on her window-pane, she lights a candle and the pair fall into each other's arms. Isobel Armstrong demonstrates how the poem's movement is

> frankly – and happily – orgasmic, from the "pushing prow" of the boat quenched in the "slushy sand" to the blue spurt of flame and "the two hearts beating, each to each".

Armstrong calls it "a poem about living in sexual time, timelessly long *and* momentary", and praises its sense of a long, serenely steady journey, with its purposive, physically relaxed movement, the soft mutedness of colour and leisurely openness to sweet sensory detail.

Browning's love lyrics cover a wide range of moods and experiences. The positive emphasis on the lovers' enjoyment of their relationship is frequently clouded with a sense of tragic irony, an implication of inevitable mortality and decay eating away at their fantasy of enduring passion. Among the most successful treatments of this theme is the one presented to us by *Love Among The Ruins*, the poem with which Browning opens his collection *Men And Women*. Written in Paris in 1853 (the Brownings had taken an apartment on the busy and fashionable Champs-Élysées), the seven stanzas return us to the Roman countryside of *Two In The Campagna*, with its landscape of sheep pasture, scattered vegetation and the crumbling remains of antique tombs. On to this background, so as to enforce our awareness of wasted achievement, baffled presumption and worldly evanescence, the poet grafts a vision of an entire ruined city, a place which once boasted its "hundred-gated circuit of a wall", a "domed and daring palace" and an amphitheatre where "the monarch and his minions and his dames/Viewed the games".

Wild nature, as in *Two In The Campagna*, has overwhelmed – or reclaimed – the city, turning it into an emblem of wasted human endeavour. In the shade of one of its towers, "by the caper over-rooted, by the gourd/Overscored,/While the patching houseleek's head of blossom winks/Through the chinks", a girl "with eager eyes and yellow hair" is waiting for the poet's embrace. It is their mutual attachment which serves to invalidate the world of marching armies, chariot races, grand designs and engineering of bridges, arches and temples, and the overall majesty and shame of empire symbolised by the ruins.

> *Shut them in,*
> *With their triumphs and their glories and the rest!*
> *Love is best.*

Seemingly positive where *Two In The Campagna* is both wistfully and cynically negative, *Love Among The Ruins* has its distinctive shading of ambiguity. What Donald Thomas calls "a mesmeric poem of visual suggestion" is inherently melancholy, fusing Browning's characteristic view of existence as something from which humanity must make the best it can with a more sombre implication of time and death closing in upon the lovers. Here, as elsewhere in his work, form and style match the overarching mood. In each stanza the exuberant gallop of one set of alternating lines is offset, or even subverted, by the brevity of the others, so as to create a sense of thwarted impulse and potential annihilation.

G.K. Chesterton praised Browning's as

the finest love poetry in the world because it does not talk about raptures and ideals and gates of heaven, but about window panes and gloves and garden walls... it is the truest of all love poetry, because it does not speak much about love.

This last point is, to say the least, debatable. Browning's gift for turning every aspect of erotic experience this way and that is indeed astonishing, as is his eagerness to locate it in a real world of everyday sights and objects, but he rarely leaves us in doubt that love forms the ultimate focus of his vision in such poems. A fascinating pendant, in this respect, to *Love Among The Ruins* is *Inapprehensiveness*, a poem written some 30 years later and published in his 1889 collection *Asolando*. As noted earlier, this portrays an actual experience, when the elderly writer clearly felt a more than merely friendly impulse towards Katherine de Kay Bronson, the rich American expatriate whose acquaintance he had made in Venice.

The arousal of amorous feelings in a twilight landscape dominated by ruins is once again Browning's theme. In *Asolo* the poet and Katherine Bronson are standing "simply friend-like side by side" looking at the medieval castle on top of the hill above the town. Her relatively commonplace musings on the plants which have rooted in its stones, and a reference to the authoritative art critic John Ruskin in this connection, are far less

interesting to Browning at this point than his own feelings towards the woman next to him. Something almost like rage overpowers him as he realises how little, if at all, she truly understands his emotional turmoil – though we should reflect that, as yet, he has not actually spoken of this himself.

> *By you stands, and may*
> *So stands unnoticed till the Judgment Day,*
> *One who, if once aware that your regard*
> *Claimed what his heart holds, – woke, as*
> > *from its sward*
> *The flower, the dormant passion, so to speak –*
> *Then what a rush of life would startling wreak*
> *Revenge on your inapprehensive stare...*

A potential good minute between the pair has been lost, but the failure here is as much his as hers. With masterly irony, Browning, in the poem's closing lines, has them resuming their bland aesthetic chit-chat, ending on the name of a newly popular writer on Italian themes:

> *"No, the book*
> *Which noticed how the wall-growths wave,"*
> *said she,*
> *"Was not by Ruskin."*
> *I said, "Vernon Lee."*

BROWNING, ASOLO AND THE TWO CATHERINES

"The most beautiful spot I ever was privileged to see," as Browning called it, the small town of Asolo, northwest of Venice, stands on a ridge forming part of the Alpine mountain range known as the Dolomites.

In the early 16th century it was given by the Venetian Republic to Caterina Cornaro, last queen of Cyprus, who held court there amid a brilliant circle of poets and men of letters. Browning spent some time at Asolo during his first visit to Italy in 1838 and its beauty made a deep impression (though unfortunately none of his letters from this first Italian trip has survived). When he returned nearly 50 years later, a little Anglo-American expatriate colony had established itself here. It included his friend Katherine de Kay Bronson. In one of

Inapprehensiveness invokes as its inspiration the contrast between "fancies that might be" and "facts that are", another central theme in Browning's comprehensive study of sexual relationships. The speaker here has a distinct notion of what he wants to happen but must, in the end, accept the triumph of a banal reality over the projections of his fantasy. In one of the best-known of the poet's early works, however, it is the imagined world which is allowed to triumph over the actual, via the most sinister of occurrences.

Porphyria's Lover was written in 1836, when its author was 24, and first appeared in a magazine

the best of his last poems, *Inapprehensiveness*, he describes with regretful irony a moment when, standing beside her on the walls of Queen Caterina's castle, he was tempted to declare his deeper feelings for Katherine Bronson, suddenly realised how pointless this would be and tried to cover his embarrassment by discussing books on Italian art and landscape instead. We know nothing, alas, of what she thought of the poem.

"This lovely Asolo, my spot of predilection in the whole world, I think" gave its name to Browning's final collection, *Asolando,* derived from the verb *asolare,* coined by Queen Caterina's favourite poet Pietro Bembo, meaning "to enjoy the delights of Asolo". The volume was published on 12 December 1889, the day its author died. He had so cherished the whole area that he planned to buy a plot of land there and build a house. "The old man," as G.K. Chesterton tells us, "could be seen continually in the lanes around Asolo, peering into hedges and whistling for the lizards." Nowadays the town's main street is called Via Robert Browning ∎

called *The Monthly Repository* (see below). Later Browning paired it with *Johannes Agricola In Meditation*, a poem written in exactly the same style about a crazed religious fanatic, under the general title "Madhouse Cells". The situation in *Porphyria's Lover* is as follows: the lover, who recounts the story for us, is waiting for his mistress to return from a supper party on a stormy evening. She comes home, takes off her bonnet, cloak and gloves, banks up the fire in the grate and sits down beside him. Mysteriously he does not respond to her as she starts to explain that "a sudden thought of one so pale/

PORPHYRIA'S SOURCES

Browning's idea for *Porphyria's Lover* derived from two contemporary sources. In 1820, his friend Bryan Waller Procter, a popular writer under the pseudonym "Barry Cornwall", had published a narrative poem, *Marcian Colonna*, in which the protagonist goes mad, murders his mistress, then sits up all night watching the dead body as if in a trance. Procter had in fact taken the hint for this from another work Browning himself had examined, *Extracts From Gosschen's Diary*, a horror story appearing two years previously in *Blackwood's Magazine*. Its author was John Wilson, friend of Wordsworth, Coleridge and De Quincey, a professor at Edinburgh University and a well-known critic, writing under the name

For love of her" has made her leave the occasion early. We are given an indication that the lover thinks Porphyria too weak to cut herself free "from pride, and vainer ties dissever/And give herself to me for ever".

The instant now assumes an absolute perfection as far as the speaker is concerned. Here the good minute offers positively horrifying possibilities as he suddenly takes the long braids of golden hair his mistress has just unpinned and strangles her with them. Following this, he props her head on his shoulder, apparently satisfied that "her darling one

Christopher North.

In the tale, a priest, visiting a condemned murderer on the eve of his execution, realises the man is insane, victim of "a despair that had no fears of this world or its terrors, but that was plunged in the abyss of eternity". The criminal acknowledges his guilt in killing his mistress: "It was I that filled her soul with bliss and with trouble – it was I alone that was privileged to take her life." The madman emphasises his "pleasure in murdering her", adding that he "grasped her by that radiant, that golden hair", that after he had stabbed her, "she never so much as gave one shriek" and that once he "laid her down upon a bank of flowers that were soon stained with her blood... My joy, my happiness was perfect... Tranquility, order, harmony and peace glittered throughout the whole universe of God." The interesting aspect of Browning's use of this material is the way in which he plays down its more violent features, laying emphasis instead on the erotic aspects and portrayal of the lover's mental instability ∎

wish" to be with him will be permanently fulfilled.

> *And thus we sit together now,*
> *And all night long we have not stirred,*
> *And yet God has not said a word!*

The combination of sex and death in *Porphyria's Lover* reflects an aspect of Browning's poetry which some contemporary readers found difficult to confront, given the prevailing image of the poet himself as a benevolent sage and philosopher. His friend Julia Wedgwood wrote forlornly to him: "I

BROWNING AND MUSIC

Music was one of Browning's deepest passions. As a child he stole downstairs from bed to listen to his mother at the piano, and, as she ceased, flung himself into her arms, whispering amid sobs, "Play, play". At a very early age he mastered the principles of harmony and counterpoint. "I was studying the grammar of music when most children are learning the multiplication table, and I know what I am talking about when I speak of music." He made musical settings of various poems, including John Donne's *Go and catch a falling star*, and at one stage even thought of composing an opera. During the years spent in London following his wife's death, Browning's friends noted how music "grew into a passion from the indulgence of which he derived some of the most beneficent influences of his wish I could apprehend the attraction of this subject to you, I thought I shared your interest in morbid anatomy." In later years the much longer *Ring and The Book* , centred on a murder story in Baroque Rome, was to test her devotion to the utmost in this respect. Other poems, such as *My Last Duchess*, the miniature Venetian drama *In A Gondola* and the grim re-telling of the Phaedra and Hippolytus story in *Artemis Prologuizes*, mirror the same preoccupation with chilling effectiveness.

Its most artful distillation occurs, more obliquely, in *A Toccata of Galuppi's*, where Browning summons

life". Though the composer Charles Villiers Stanford, meeting him at Cambridge in 1884, observed that he "talked most and knew least about music", others, such as the great violinist Joseph Joachim and the conductor Charles Hallé, were impressed by "the extraordinary range of his acquaintance with the works of great and even of obscure composers".

The latter provided inspiration for a whole range of poems. Apart from Baldassare Galuppi, whose work, rediscovered during the 20th century, was hardly known at all in Browning's day, we meet Georg Josef Vogler, another 18th-century musician – the poet considered *Abt Vogler* (1864) one of his finest achievements – Charles Avison, a musical theorist from the same period, and an imaginary composer, *Master Hugues of Saxe-Gotha*. This last work, imitating a musical fugue and spoken by the organist playing it, is a subtle yet also impassioned attack on the concept of music as a mere matter of abstract systems without reference to the world of human feeling ∎

up the spirit of 18th-century Venice via the keyboard music of its finest composers, Baldassare Galuppi (1706-85). At first glance the poem's subject seems to be the way in which we can find a closer connection with a vanished culture via the different works of art it has left behind. Playing or listening to Galuppi's compositions leads the speaker (who tells us that he "was never out of England") to forge an imaginative link with the decadent, pleasure-loving world of the Venetian Republic in its last phase of existence before being conquered by Napoleon's French army in 1797.

> *Did young people take their pleasure when the*
> *sea was warm in May?*
> *Balls and masks begun at midnight, burning ever*
> *to mid-day,*
> *When they made up fresh adventures for the*
> *morrow, do you say?*

With wonderful stealth Browning gradually forces on us the realisation that this is more than simply an essay in period re-creation or a chance to display, yet again, the staggering breadth of his reading and erudition. Part of the poem's impact, admittedly, arises from the witty dichotomy between the attitude of the speaker, a bluff, arrogant and decidedly insular Englishman, who resents the insidious impact on him of Galuppi's toccata (a kind of free-flowing keyboard piece), and the refinement and sophistication of the Venice which gave birth to such music. Yet *A Toccata of Galuppi's* gradually folds into its texture the broader, less personal issue of how much our sense of being alive is made real by the overhanging shadow of mortality. In summoning up his vision of Galuppi's Venetian world, Browning uses the power of the question mark, in the stanza quoted above, to enhance our awareness of its uncertainty and impermanence.

Beautiful and elegant as the 18th-century figures are, with their sword, mask and fan, who listen to the composer playing, "stately at the clavichord", these Venetians are as doomed as the civilization they represent:

*Then they left you for their pleasure: till in due
time, one by one,
Some with lives that came to nothing, some with
deeds as well undone,
Death stepped tacitly and took them where they
never see the sun.*

Erotic dalliance cannot stall the Grim Reaper's advance. Venice, as always in Browning's own era, becomes a symbol of the vanity of human achievement and aspiration.

*As for Venice and her people, merely born to bloom
and drop,
Here on earth they bore their fruitage, mirth and*

> *folly were the crop.*
> *What of soul was left, I wonder, when the kissing*
> *had to stop?*

Emotion experienced through the act of love, by seizing our opportunities for connection with one another, forms a vital link between a whole series of Browning poems. A contrasting awareness, as in *A Toccata of Galuppi's*, that everything else in life is vain and perishable inspired one of his most piquant and skilfully-wrought lyrics, *Youth and Art*, in which the poet shares with us his rueful amusement at the ironies within the situation portrayed.

The speaker here is a woman who, in her younger days, training to be an opera singer, shared lodgings with a student sculptor, "you a sparrow on the housetop lonely,/I a lone she-bird of his feather". The pair of them work energetically enough at their respective arts, though, as she admits:

> *I earned no more by a warble*
> *Than you by a sketch in plaster;*
> *You wanted a piece of marble,*
> *I needed a music master.*

The two students, more or less content, for the time being, with their bohemian lifestyle, are inevitably conscious of each other's physical attractiveness. It's here that a markedly un-Victorian Browning shows his hand, an audacious one at that. How many

other mainstream English poets in 1860 would have
allowed their heroine to admit that

> *And I – soon managed to find*
> *Weak points in the flower-fence facing,*
> *Was forced to put up a blind*
> *And be safe in my corset-lacing?*

Later the sexual element is flagged up with overt
symbolism:

> *For spring bade the sparrows pair,*
> *And the boys and girls gave guesses,*
> *And stalls in our street looked rare*
> *With bulrush and watercresses.*

Sparrows were birds traditionally identified
with vigorous mating activity, and the two plants
mentioned in the stanza's last line do duty for male
and female genitalia.

The speaker's point, however – and we should
reflect on how indelicate many Victorians would
have considered the entire discourse in the mouth of
someone who, by the end of the poem, has become
a respectable lady – is that these potential young
lovers never got it together. Each in their chosen
artistic field has joined Browning's gallery of fakes
and failures. Their particular "good minute" has
been sacrificed and the same moral ambiguity clouds
the sardonic ending of *Youth and Art* as we find

playing around the conclusion of *The Statue and the Bust* :

> *Each life unfulfilled, you see;*
> *It hangs still, patchy and scrappy:*
> *We have not sighed deep, laughed free,*
> *Starved, feasted, despaired – been happy.*
> *And nobody calls you a dunce,*
> *And people suppose me clever:*
> *This could but have happened once,*
> *And we missed it, lost it for ever.*

Why did Italy matter to Browning?

No reading of Browning's poetry can ignore – or afford to ignore – the significance of Italy for the poet. He made extended tours there in 1838 and 1844, lived in Florence from 1847 to 1861, began a series of further visits from 1878 onwards and during his final years spent long periods living in Venice and the Veneto. It was in Venice that he died on 12 December 1889. Though he himself privately maintained rather a scornful attitude towards contemporary Italian writers, the country of his adoption took him to its heart, treating him and Elizabeth Barrett Browning as honorary citizens. The houses in which they lived are marked by memorial plaques and there are streets and squares named after them in Florence, Rome and Asolo.

Browning was clearly aware that the inspiration for much of his finest achievement as a poet had been kindled by an absorption with Italy and things Italian. As the critic Ian Jack has remarked of Browning's return to England following Elizabeth's death: "It is tempting to say that when Browning left Italy he left his genius behind him." Jack goes on to quote what he calls "a curiously revealing passage" from a letter to Browning's close friend Isa Blagden, written in 1866:

> I agree with you & always did, as to the uninterestingness of the Italians individually, as thinking, originating souls: I never read a line in a modern Italian book that was of use to me, - never saw a flash of poetry come out of an Italian *word*: in art, in action, *yes*, – not in the region of ideas: I always said they *are* poetry, [they] don't and can't *make* poetry... my liking for Italy was always a selfish one, –I felt alone with my own soul there.

For most of Browning's early life, Italy was not a unified nation state, but merely, in the famous words of the Austrian politician Clemens von Metternich, "a geographical expression". The Italian peninsula was divided among a variety of kingdoms and duchies, with a sizeable portion given over to the so-called "States of the Church", ruled from Rome by the Pope and his cardinals. Each of these territories

TEN FACTS
ABOUT THE BROWNINGS

1.

At a dinner party on 7 April 1889, at the home
of Browning's friend, the artist Rudolf Lehmann,
a recording was made on a white wax cylinder
by Edison's British representative, George Gouraud. In
the recording, which still exists, Browning recites part of
How They Brought the Good News from Ghent to Aix (and
can be heard apologising when he forgets the words!).
The recording was played in 1890 on the anniversary of
his death, said to be the first time anyone's voice "had been
heard from beyond the grave."

2.

Browning was precocious – he had written his first book
poetry by the age of 12, entitled *Incondita*, though this was
later destroyed when his parents failed to find a publisher.
He is said to have read all 50 volumes of the *Biographie
Universelle* and learned Latin, Greek, French and Italian
by the time he was 14.

3.

One of the Brownings' more unusual encounters was
with Daniel Douglas Home - a spiritualist medium
who enjoyed great celebrity during the late Victorian
era. (He was born in 1833, and died in 1886.) Home
conducted séances in many wealthy households, and
boasted powers of levitation as well as resistance to fire

James Jackson Jarves, an art critic raised in America, relayed enthusiastic reports of Home's achievements back to Mrs Browning. "Mr Jarves told me the other day... that twenty or thirty persons, of his own acquaintance, have been brought to abjure atheism and materialism by these manifestations," she wrote to her sister. While Robert had maintained that "if it's spiritual, I'm inclined to think it's devilish", Elizabeth took this condemnation as "the most cruel conclusion I ever heard. I protest against any such conclusion".

4.

On 10th January 1845, Browning wrote to Elizabeth. Hitherto their only acquaintance had been through poetry. In *Lady Geraldine's Courtship*, two years before, she had referred to his *Bells and Pomegranates*, "which, if cut deep down the middle,/ Shows a heart within blood-tinctured,/ Of a veined humanity". Bertram, the speaker at this point, talks of Browning in the same breath as Wordsworth and Tennyson. The compliment was not lost on Browning; memorably, his first letter to her begins "I love your verses with all my heart, dear Miss Barrett."

They were married in September 1846, and a few days later eloped to Italy where they lived until her death in 1861.

5.

Rudolf Besier's 1930 play, *The Barretts of Wimpole Street*, dramatised the courtship of Browning and Elizabeth. The conflict centres around Elizabeth's overbearing father, who was reluctant that she should marry. It transferred to Broadway in 1931, where it ran for 370 performances. Subsequent film and TV adaptations have starred Fredric March, John Neville, Bill Travers (see p.111) and Jeremy Brett in the role of Browning.

6.
John Lennon's *Grow Old With Me* was inspired by Browning's poem *Rabbi Ben Ezra*. It appears on Lennon's album *Milk and Honey*.

7.
His wife was a more popular poet than he was during his lifetime. Elizabeth Barrett Browning, née Moulton-Barrett, was a precocious classical scholar, composing an epic poem on the Battle of Marathon at the age of 14. Her first widely published work, *An Essay on Mind, and other Poems*, followed in 1826. She translated Aeschylus's *Prometheus Bound* over the course of 12 days in 1833, though later wrote that it "should have been thrown into the fire afterwards - the only means of giving it a little warmth". Some of Elizabeth's best-known poetry comes from the period leading up to her marriage, including her *Sonnets from the Portuguese*, which contains one of the most famous opening lines in English love poetry: "How do I love thee? Let me count the ways."

8.
Elizabeth spent long periods of her life as an invalid. Prescribed morphine since she was 14, at the time of her first meeting with Browning she had not left the house

for five years. In their early letters of courtship, the couple likened romantic dependency to Elizabeth's reliance upon drugs. "May I call you my morphine?" he asked her- to which she replied, the next day: "Can I be as good for you as morphine is for me, I wonder, even at the cost of being as bad also?- Can't you leave me off without risking your life- nor go on with me without running the hazards of all poison?"

9.

Casa Guidi, the house that became the Brownings' permanent residence from 1847, is believed to be the final resting place of Flush, Elizabeth's beloved cocker spaniel. He is immortalised in her own poetry - *To Flush, Flush or Faunus?*- as well as Virginia Woolf's *Flush: A Biography*.

10.

Percy Bysshe Shelley (1792-1822) was a decisive influence on Browning from the age of 15. From Shelley, Stefan Hawlin notes, Browning imbibed the virtues of "atheism, vegetarianism [and] political radicalism". His admiration was tempered in later life by learning of Shelley's conduct towards his first wife. In 1885 Browning wrote that "For myself, I painfully contrast my notions of Shelley the man and Shelley, well, even the poet, with what they were sixty years ago, when I only had his works, for a certainty, and took his character on trust." When Browning's estate came up for auction in May 1913, it included a wrapped and labelled flower, picked from Shelley's grave.

had different laws, monetary and revenue systems. Foreign travellers, whatever their eagerness to visit Italy, complained incessantly of the difficulties involved in crossing a whole series of frontiers en route from one town to another. In the course of the journey, unless substantial bribes were paid to the various customs officials, tourists might expect to have their luggage examined as many as seven or eight times.

The dream of many Italians – though by no means all of them – was that Italy should at length become a single united country, and during the early 19th century a groundswell of revolutionary activity had begun to gather momentum in various cities, Naples, Rome and Venice among them. There were serious political upheavals throughout Italy in 1821, 1830 and during the early 1840s. What Italians call the Risorgimento – literally "resurgence" of a suppressed patriotic spirit – made the established regimes (most of them oppressive police states) increasingly nervous. When the newly married Robert and Elizabeth Browning arrived in Italy in 1846, a major revolution seemed inevitable, though at that stage many people believed this could be headed off if individual sovereigns such as the King of Naples or the Duke of Modena could be persuaded to make a few concessions to liberal opinion and relax the stifling controls on the press, education and free speech.

The Brownings inevitably found themselves

Palazzo Rezzonico, where Browning died in 1889. He died on the day that Asolando *was published*

swept up in this moment of – as it turned out –
misplaced optimism when they settled in the
territories of Grand Duke Leopold II of Tuscany,
first in Pisa, then in Florence. Robert and Elizabeth,
however, developed markedly different attitudes
to the nationalist struggle, which broke out into
armed revolution across the whole of Italy during
the late spring of 1848. While his wife flung herself
passionately into the cause of Italian liberty with
her extended two-part poem *Casa Guidi Windows*
(1850), Browning, for his part, though broadly
supporting the central impulse of the Risorgimento

towards Italian nationhood, adopted a more sidelong, sometimes openly sceptical approach to the momentous episodes unfolding around him and towards those concerned with making them happen.

Hence comparatively few of his poems are directly concerned with the Italian revolution and the emotions which it aroused. Even the most obviously *risorgimentale* of them, *The Italian in England,* as Ian Jack points out, "is as much concerned with the character of the speaker as with the story that is told".

Admittedly it may have been suggested by the figure of the great revolutionary ideologue Giuseppe Mazzini, a political refugee during the 1840s and personally known to Browning while living in London. The poet's earliest biographer Alexandra Sutherland Orr, in her 1885 *Handbook to the Works of Robert Browning*, notes that "Mr Browning is proud to remember that Mazzini informed him he had read this poem to certain of his fellow-exiles in England to show how an Englishman could sympathise with them".

Spoken by a fugitive from the Austrians, whose empire at that time included the whole of northern Italy from the Alps to the River Po, *The Italian in England* deals with the fundamental issue of how much an individual's dedication to a sacred political cause should be allowed to overshadow his personal life as an ordinary human being. The revolutionary fugitive, while escaping "Austria's bloodhounds", has been aided by a peasant girl whose beauty and heroism have clearly challenged his ability to suppress private emotions. The end of the poem acknowledges that not even the most obsessive activist can deny the reality of love:

I think then, I should wish to stand
This evening in that dear, lost land,
Over the sea the thousand miles,
And know if yet that woman smiles
With the calm smile.

Yet, even as the speaker adds that he would have liked to

sit there for an hour about,
Then kiss her hand once more, and lay
Mine on her head, and go my way...

he is forced to admit that he and his fellow revolutionaries have more important business in hand:

So much for idle wishing – how
It steals the time! To business now.

The American critic E.D.H. Johnson, in his essay "Authority and the Rebellious Heart" (1952), sees *The Italian in England* as one of those Browning poems in which, for better or worse, "the protagonist must make his decision between the practical inducements to worldly success and a lonely integrity of spirit" – precisely the choice, indeed, which Andrea del Sarto is shown as being morally and spiritually so ill-equipped to make. In another Risorgimento poem, *The Patriot,* Browning saw just how fatal an outcome such a decision might have had in the aftermath of Italy's 1848 revolutions. This is a much more cynical affair than *The Italian in England*, which precedes it by almost a decade. Here the writer contrasts the jubilant reception of Italian freedom fighters, symbolised as it is by "roses, roses all the way", church bells ringing and cheering crowds, with the near emptiness of the streets as, in due course, the patriot himself, having "leaped at the sun/To give it my loving friends to keep", is led to execution. He sees this as nothing worse than a punishment for his own vanity in making his gesture of revolution in the first place.

Browning's most effective Italian poems are either those set in the historical past, such as *Fra Lippo Lippi, My Last Duchess* and *A Toccata of Galuppi's*, or those that reflect his intensely pictorial grasp of the Italy which surrounded him. A potent example of this visual evocation of the country he loved so well is offered to us in *The Englishman in Italy*, a work which was published as a companion piece to *The Italian in England*, but which has absolutely no connection to it in form, mood or idiom.

One of Browning's most exuberant tributes to the beauty of the Italian scene, the poem is almost the only one inspired by a landscape of the south, the region around Naples, as opposed to those of Tuscany, the Veneto and the Roman Campagna which provide the backgrounds elsewhere. Amid the lush beauty of the fertile plain around the town of Sorrento, we are shown Italy at her most abundantly picturesque. The vines are laden with grape, pomegranates are "chapping and splitting in halves on the tree", figs are spread to dry on the housetops and a fisherman displays a basket full of "pink and grey jellies, your sea-fruit". The whole atmosphere is one of plenty and profusion. There will be lasagne, aubergines and mozzarella for supper, washed down with "weak wine" from a green glass flask.

We hear, as well as see, this southern Italy so wondrously recreated for us in Browning's tumbling spondees. The sirocco, the fierce southern wind off the Mediterranean, rattles down the olives and medlars, a mule neighs across the valley and the fisherman's children, "as naked/and brown as his shrimps", run screaming around him. Nobody had ever written like this before, certainly not an Italian poet. As Browning was surely aware, *The Englishman in Italy* opens up a new kind of discourse in the form of a densely localised physicality, so that the whole panorama becomes realised via sensory experience. The work issued a challenge to his contemporaries they were notably reluctant to accept and it needed another half century before English writers began investigating this kind of poetic world on their own initiative. It is only fair to add, nevertheless, that Browning went on to write few other poems in which human beings matter less than the components of the material world surrounding them.

From a purely stylistic aspect, a more appropriate companion for *The Englishman in Italy* is *Up At A Villa – Down in the City*, subtitled "As Distinguished by an Italian Person of Quality". Here Browning both celebrates and mocks the land of his adoption. Italians, unlike the English, with their passion for rural living, have an uneasy relationship with the countryside. For centuries peasant farmers in many parts of Italy lived wretched lives, sometimes in a state of serfdom, until the growth of the major cities following unification encouraged thousands of agricultural workers to seek employment in factories or else to emigrate to America. Urban life in any case, since the Middle Ages, had always seemed more attractive to Italians of all classes for its guarantees of security, affluence and sociability.

The aristocracy needed, however, to make sure that the landed estates funding its city lifestyle were being properly managed, so every summer the great families left the towns for their country houses. Such an exodus also afforded an opportunity for the palaces to be thoroughly cleaned and for those making the move to breathe healthier air during a season marked by the spread of epidemics and infections. This annual migration was known as *la villeggiatura* – the visit to the villa.

Browning's adopted persona in *Up At A Villa – Down In The City* is a Tuscan nobleman on *villeggiatura*. Characteristically he longs to be back in town, with "Something to see, by Bacchus, something to hear, at least!" instead of having to stay at "our villa, stuck like the horns of a bull/Just on a mountain's edge as bare as the creature's skull". We learn immediately that he cannot afford to move back into town (the family has evidently rented out or even lost its palazzo) and the whole poem is essentially an expression of frustrated yearning for the fun, clatter and bustle of streets and squares as opposed to the unvarying rhythms of a lonely life among woods and fields. The landscape Browning celebrates so lavishly elsewhere here becomes charged with a sense of effort and monotony. Marooned on his estate, the nobleman finds no charm in "the faint grey olive trees" or in "yon cypress that points like death's lean lifted forefinger". The winter fades too slowly, the summer arrives too fast, the insects are too noisy, some of the crops are smelly, others don't grow fast enough.

The glimpses offered of city living, on the other hand, show just how accurately Browning intuited the fundamental motors of Italian life, its gregariousness, its need for variety, its emphasis on the visual and the significance of being seen in streets, cafés and shops and not having to spend long stretches of the day indoors. "You watch who crosses and gossips, who saunters, who hurries by", the local stagecoach rattles into town with passengers, letters and news and the travelling doctor "gives pills, lets blood, draws teeth". A passing religious procession features a holy image of

> our Lady borne smiling and smart
> With a pink gauze gown all spangles, and
> > seven swords stuck in her heart!

We know, all the same, that the anonymous aristocrat, childlike and not especially sophisticated,

THE RING AND THE BOOK

———————

A traditional epic poem features elements such as a heroic quest, a hazardous voyage or a story mingling love and warfare. The forces of destiny, enchantment or supernatural intervention by gods and goddesses may each play a major role in the narrative's unfolding events. Browning never tried his hand at anything of this sort or indeed seriously contemplated doing so. To many Victorian readers however, *The Ring And The Book,* first issued in four instalments between November 1868 and February 1869, counted as the next best thing. The source of this singular work, essentially a novel in verse (Browning had originally offered the subject to Anthony Trollope), was a book, "small-quarto size, will somehow never make it back to the city for whose hubbub and excitement he pines.

Ian Jack calls *Up At A Villa – Down In The City* "one of the most lighthearted of all Browning's poems, a poem that is Chaucerian in the skill of the characterisation and in the joy that the poet takes in the character whom he is so memorably endowing with a voice". The speaker, as Jack says, "is as fascinated by the human scene as is Fra Lippo Lippi, but much less intelligent" and these qualities are mirrored in the nature of the versification. Browning uses the hexameter rhythm he would have mastered when studying Greek and Latin poetry as a boy.

part print, part manuscript", picked up off a street stall in Florence. It contained the details of a 17th-century murder trial, involving Pompilia, daughter of a Roman whore, whose adoptive parents married her off to Count Guido, a down-at-heel aristocrat. When she became pregnant by her lover, the priest Giuseppe Caponsacchi, Guido murdered her, a crime for which he was subsequently tried and executed.

"The Old Yellow Book", as Browning called the trial record, is transmogrified, in his poem, into a multiple narrative, its events scrutinised from different points of view via a sequence of dramatic monologues wound up by the poet's own commentary. As well as the voices of Pompilia, Guido and Giuseppe, we hear those of the Roman populace, both high-born and lowly, of the wily, self-serving lawyers for either side, and of the Pope himself, Innocent XII, on whose shoulders responsibility for the final verdict rested. This experiment in diffuse perspectives is not original

Jack notes that these "rush along in the headlong manner of breathless, gossiping conversation" and the irregular number of lines from stanza to stanza (three, four, six, four, five etc.), as well as a variable rhyme scheme, serves to "enhance the effect of a torrent of chatter".

It is impossible to doubt the strength and sincerity of Browning's attachment to Italy or the potency of the various kinds of inspiration he drew from it, but critics tend to divide on the issue of how much modern Italy, fervently engaged in the business of trying to turn itself into a single country, meant to him as something more than a place where he could "feel alone with his own soul". Barbara Melchiori,

to the poem – novelists had already made use of it in such works as Wilkie Collins's *The Moonstone* and Charles Dickens's *Bleak House* – but no poet before Browning had employed to such elaborate and complex effect.

The Ring And The Book has been seen both as Browning's masterpiece, "the most precious and profound spiritual treasure that England has produced since the days of Shakespeare", and as his most accomplished failure.

The painter-poet Dante Gabriel Rossetti told his friend William Allingham that it reinforced his idea that too much contact with reality had a bad effect on Browning, but G.K. Chesterton called it "the great epic of free speech". Most critics have seen the whole achievement as an important reflection of the ways in which the writer's own era faced the challenges of moral relativism and increasingly complex notions of truth as handled by an inspired and sophisticated creative artist ∎

for example, herself Italian, is eager to underline how quintessentially English the poet's way of life remained during his various residences in Tuscany, Asolo and Venice. Robert and Elizabeth's friends, while they lived in Florence, tended to include members of the increasingly influential Anglo-American community, whose influence can still be felt in the modern city, even if this expatriate presence became substantially diminished during the latter part of the 20th century. Italians, when they did impinge on the lives of such figures as the sculptor William Whetmore Storey, the journalist Thomas Adolphus Trollope (brother of novelist Anthony) or Browning's friend Isabella Blagden, generally took the form of servants, art dealers or anglophile members of the local aristocracy. There were English tea-rooms, an English bookshop and an English cemetery, and it would have been possible for many of the community not to have to learn more than a smattering of kitchen Italian or enough of the language to make themselves understood in shops – though to do the Brownings justice, each of them spoke the language more than adequately.

Melchiori maintains that while Browning's sympathy with the Risorgimento may have found expression in *The Italian in England,* the poem was in fact written before he took up long-term residence in Italy and that by the time this commenced, he, unlike Elizabeth, "no longer wanted to become involved". What Italy really meant to him, Melchiori suggests, had everything to do with the stimulus offered to his creativity by the changes in his own life brought about through marriage to Elizabeth Barrett and almost nothing to do with the dramatically shifting realities in the lives of ordinary Italians during the 1840s and 1850s. When, following his wife's death, he told William Whetmore Storey "If you knew – but you do know and can conceive how precious every mud-splash on the house walls of Rome is", Melchiori believes that "there is no doubt that at this time Italy was closely connected in his mind with his married life, and that the nostalgia he felt was part of his bereavement".

His real Italy, she implies, was constructed almost solely from books, "the Italy that he found in his library, the Italy of the past". It reflected that ability to distance himself from his immediate surroundings which Henry James identified in his story *The Private Life*, but by the same token it gave the poet a fuller opportunity for the kind of imaginative transference to another time, place or persona which is his outstanding gift as an artist. This is not to say that Browning necessarily assumes the tastes and attitudes, in their entirety, of whatever Italian characters he chooses to evoke. As Melchiori says,

the Italian painters about whom Browning is writing are being used as vehicles for his own ideas, and, for all his careful documentation, it is a mistake to consider him as an authority on Italian art.

A contrary view of Browning's Italian experience is presented by Matthew Reynolds in *The Realms Of Verse* (2001), subtitled "English Poetry In A Time Of Nation-Building". In a chapter on "Browning's Alien Pages" the critic presents a telling case for a powerful subtext of Italian political reference running all the way through the 50 poems gathered in *Men And Women*, the collection generally regarded as its author's most dazzling performance. Reynolds identifies oppression in its various forms, psychological, marital, religious or social, as a binding theme here. He shows us how different kinds of domestic tyranny, fantasies of control and "enjoyment of quiescence" in works seemingly unrelated to the Italian scene, such as *Evelyn Hope*, *Mesmerism* and *A Woman's Last Word,* can be linked to the impact of the absolutist regimes ruling the states of Italy in the crucial decade before unification, the very era when the Brownings chose to settle there. According to this interpretation, even a poem like *Two In The Campagna*, for all its apparent focus on sexual intimacy, possesses a political resonance. The disillusioned lover in the poem

> not only is, but recognizes himself to be, living at a
> time in which the "infinite" is strongly
> distinguished from the "finite" and the two seem
> not to meet; in which, therefore, it has become
> impossible to feel at one with the State, with

another person, or even with yourself.

We can easily take issue with this, as also with Reynolds's claim that Browning, "as he turned Italian subjects into 'pure poetry', representing vigorous Italian characters and vivid Italian scenery in his writing, must have had a thought somewhere in his mind that he was helping to bring Italy into cultural existence, and that he was thereby in some not very well-defined way supporting the Risorgimento". The reality probably has more to do with the poet's creative opportunism than with Italy's cultural existence or his support for its nationalist revolt. He and Elizabeth had, after all, as Barbara Melchiori reminds us, first moved to Italy simply because the climate of Pisa had been recommended to her, while still ostensibly an invalid, by her doctor. Had he recommended the Swiss Alps she would surely have gone there instead. Browning had already drawn on Italian inspirations in *Pippa Passes,* based on the experience of his trip to the Veneto in 1838, and in *Sordello,* the long poem published in 1840 whose critical reception was so disastrous as to traumatise him for the remainder of his literary career.

What Italy now offered him was an apparently infinite extension of those raw materials which had brought such vitality to outstanding works written in the immediate aftermath of the *Sordello* debacle, poems such as *The Englishman in Italy* and *The*

An 1870 portrait by Edward Clifford. Evelyn Waugh owned this picture and gave it its current title, Evelyn Hope, *after Browning's poem*

Bishop Orders His Tomb At Saint Praxed's Church. This latter is both a bravura exercise in the dramatic monologue genre and a fascinating example of the way in which its author's cultural saturation in the life and art of a historical period can create an authenticity which sometimes seems almost more powerfully convincing than those genuine voices resonating from the era itself. Scholars have felt that they know the eponymous Bishop so well that they can actually identify him as a historical figure – it has been suggested, for example, that he is Cardinal Ippolito d'Este, uncle of that very same Duke of Ferrara later portrayed in *My Last Duchess.*

The Bishop is one of those Browning characters in whom we come to cherish the frankness with which their monstrous imperfections are laid bare. On his deathbed he commands his so-called nephews – soon identified as his sons – to raise him a monument according to his specifications, using particular varieties of marble and placing it in a precisely determined spot within the Roman church of Santa Prassede (the Bishop mistakenly identifies the saint, a female martyr of the second century AD, as a man). The rascally old cleric is preoccupied, not with the

HOME IN FLORENCE – "A TORRENT ON STRAW"

"We keep to our plans of wandering up and down," Elizabeth Barrett Browning wrote to her sister from Pisa in 1846, "it is necessary for my health and convenient; and we like, both of us, this way of living, free from domestic cares and the ordering and cooking of dinners." A few months later she and Robert moved to Florence, where they settled in the house on Via Maggio known as Casa Guidi. This stood not far from Palazzo Pitti, nowadays a world-famous art gallery but then the residence of the Grand Duke of Tuscany. Here they were to live for the next 15 years, with occasional trips to Paris and London and extended visits to Rome. The household was Anglo-Italian: Elizabeth, on her elopement with Robert, was accompanied by her faithful maid Liza Wilson, who enjoyed baking scones for the Brownings, but the cooking was mostly done by local chef Alessandro, whom they considered "a master, state of his immortal soul and its likely damnation, but by memories of his beautiful mistress, mother of the "nephews", and by his ferocious rivalry with a certain "old Gandolf", already buried in the church.

The world Browning conjures up for us is that of late 15th and early 16th-century Italy, the age of Lippo Lippi and Andrea del Sarto, a high Renaissance in which wealth and power found expression in the commission and collecting of works of art and in rediscovering and reinterpreting the culture and ideals of Greco-Roman antiquity.

---

an artist!" because he knew how to make beefsteak pies, apple dumplings and bread-and-butter pudding (no local pasta dishes for English poets, evidently).

Here in Casa Guidi, on 9 March, 1849, while Italy was in the throes of revolution, their son Robert Wiedemann Browning, known as "Pen", was born, and in this same house, on 29 June, 1861, Elizabeth died in her husband's arms, after exclaiming: "My Robert – my heavens, my beloved ! Our lives are held by God !" The day after she died, the sculptor William Wetmore Story and his wife Emelyn listened as Browning, looking around the drawing room, declared: "The cycle is complete. Here we came fifteen years ago; here Pen was born; here Ba [Elizabeth's family nickname] wrote her poems for Italy... Every day she used to walk with me or drive with me, and once even walked to Bellosguardo [a Florentine hilltop] and back; that was when she was strongest. Little by little, I see now that distance was lessened, the active out-doors life restricted, until walking had finally ceased... Looking back at these past few years I see that we have been all the time walking over a torrent on straw." ∎

Most often quoted from *The Bishop Orders His Tomb* in this connection are the lines:

> *And have I not Saint Praxed's ear to pray*
> *Horses for ye, and brown Greek manuscripts,*
> *And mistresses with great smooth marbly limbs?*

It was the great art critic John Ruskin who famously praised this passage in his book *Modern Painters*:

> I know no other piece of modern English, prose or poetry, in which there is so much told, as in these lines, of the Renaissance spirit, – its worldliness, inconsistency, pride, hypocrisy, ignorance of itself, love of art, of luxury, and of good Latin.

He acknowledged that Browning had anticipated much of his own writing, in the highly influential *Stones Of Venice*, on the art and architecture of the period.

By the same token it ought not greatly to matter to us if the Church of Saint Praxed, as imagined by Browning, bears no obvious resemblance to the actual building in Rome and the latter contains no monument to a Renaissance bishop, in precious marbles or any other kind of stone. The important element here is not authenticity in the literal sense, but the poet's imaginative gift for bringing an entire world and its individual inhabitants, even "a disgusting old reprobate" like the Bishop, to such vivid and abundant life. Thus it may indeed be possible for us to talk about somewhere called "Browning's Italy", as opposed to the genuine article, and feel that the former, after its fashion, possesses as much validity as the latter.

What cannot be denied, even by critics who see an Italian thematic emphasis in the poet's work as simply an oblique species of cultural colonialism, is his personal devotion to Italy as a source of spiritual nourishment and unending artistic inspiration. The sincerity of this attachment is enshrined for us in *De Gustibus*, a poem written in 1854 which finds Browning in the unusual situation of telling readers something about himself. Its title is drawn from the Latin proverb "De gustibus nihil est disputandum" – "About tastes there's nothing to be argued over" – suggesting that not everybody is likely to share the writer's enthusiasm here.

The opening section deliberately employs the most hackneyed rhymes, across a rhythmically-fragmented scatter of 13 lines, to dismiss the image of England as having any real significance for Browning. In the second, once arrived in Italy, a genuine fervour takes possession of him, whether he finds himself in

> *a castle, precipice-encurled,*
> *In a gash of the wind-grieved Apennine*

or

In a sea-side house to the farther south
Where the baked cicalas die of drouth.

In the latter setting he watches a scorpion climbing up the frescoed wall as a barefooted girl throws "green-flesh melons" on the marble floor and brings news that the King of Naples has been shot at.

"She hopes they have not caught the felons." Perhaps, after all, the Risorgimento was not as far from Browning's interests as some critics think. Maybe the very same mixture, reflected in these closing lines, of art, food, colour, people and politics is what guaranteed his profound allegiance, throughout his life, to what, earlier in the poem, he calls "the land of lands".

How should we read *Childe Roland*?

Childe Roland To The Dark Tower Came is the most famously enigmatic of all Browning's poems. First published in *Men And Women* in 1855, it was probably written three years earlier and takes its title from a line in Shakespeare's *King Lear*. Edgar, a fugitive from the intrigues against him by his bastard brother Edmund, has disguised himself as a semi-imbecile vagabond or "village idiot" called Poor Tom. Encountering Lear wandering through the stormy night, he joins the mad king's entourage and, as they all retreat into the hovel, mutters a snatch of an old ballad:

> *"Childe Roland to the dark tower came;*
> *His word was still 'Fie, foh and fum,*
> *I smell the blood of a British man.'"*

Shakespeare scholars have failed to trace the origin of the first of these lines, but the other two belong to the old tale of Jack the Giant-Killer, where they are nowadays better known in the form "Fee, fie, foh, fum/I smell the blood of an Englishman." This traditional folk legend, with its pantomime variant *Jack And The Beanstalk,* together with references to Sir Thomas Malory's *Morte d'Arthur*, John Bunyan's *The Pilgrim's Progress*, Dante's *Inferno* and various poems by William Wordsworth, have all been identified as sources for Browning's *Childe Roland.*

The writer himself, however, was notably unforthcoming about possible interpretations of a work which, while hinting at a whole world of epic adventure, chivalric exploits, symbolism and allegory, is full of those purely mysterious, unexplained elements with which storytellers have always enjoyed puzzling their readers and listeners. It deliberately avoids the rooted actuality so characteristic of Browning's other dramatic monologues. What precisely is happening in *Childe Roland To The Dark Tower Came,* what has occurred before the poem opens and what will take place after the speaker reaches the Dark Tower itself in the last line?

The plot of the poem appears to run as follows. Childe Roland, who has spent many years searching for the Dark Tower, has encountered an old man who sets him on his way there, but whom he also appears to mistrust. Roland knows that many other knights before him have gone in search of the Tower but failed in their quest. He starts to ride across the barren plain, uninhabited by anything except "one stiff blind horse" and remembers friends he has lost through their own disgrace. Fording a sinister little river, he sticks his spear into something, but isn't sure if this is a water-rat or a baby. On the other side he discovers evidence of a recent battle and comes across a curious machine "with rusty teeth of steel", whose purpose is unclear.

Increasingly the landscape grows more hideous, with its "stark black dearth", "substances like boils", a cleft in an oak tree "like a distorted mouth that splits rim/Gaping at death" and the sudden apparition of a great black bird, which Roland believes is "perchance the guide I sought". As the mountains begin to close in around the plain, he realises that this is where the Tower must be:

The round, squat turret, blind as the fool's heart,
Built of brown stone, without a counterpart

and at length he seems to hear the hillsides ringing with

Edward Burne-Jones's Childe Roland to the Tower Came, *1861*

> *Names in my ears*
> *Of all the lost adventurers, my peers.*

As these figures actually make an appearance, watching him "in a sheet of flame", Roland blows his horn. The last words of the poem are indeed Edgar's "Childe Roland to the Dark Tower came".

Few writers on Browning seem to have detected the presence in the poem of elements from one of the stories included in *The Arabian Nights*. This tale, *The Speaking Bird*, is not an original part of the ancient Oriental collection, but was added from a Persian source to translations made from the Arabic text during the 18th century. In it two princes set out on a quest, during which they meet a wise old man, who urges them not to continue. When they insist on pressing forward, he warns them that a mountain which they have to climb is fraught with danger because of the black stones littering its slopes. The stones will start to whisper and mutter as soon as the princes start their ascent. If they take any notice of these discouraging voices they will never return. Both men nevertheless fail to heed these instructions and are themselves turned to stone. It is left to their valiant sister to brave the mountainside and capture the speaking bird who lives on its summit. Browning made use of the idea of failed questors doomed to transformation, found in many similar myths and legends, of the mysterious voices and of the old man whom the hero or heroine meets on the way. What he deliberately avoided was the happy ending usually achieved in such stories. It is not absolutely certain that Childe Roland will die once arrived at the Dark Tower and having raised the slughorn to his lips, but most readers assume this to be inevitable.

So how do we interpret this doom-laden saga of apparently fruitless heroic endeavour? Critical attention on *Childe Roland To The Dark Tower Came* was always keen from its earliest publication, and modern writers on Browning have intensified the discourse in the light of 20th-century interest in symbolism and the world of dreams. The Canadian critic William Cadbury, for example, writing on

Browning's "Lyric And Anti-Lyric Forms", detects significance in the disorder of the landscape Roland traverses after having forded the river in Stanza XXVII. The prospect offers

> consistent reductions of the possibility of meaning and the place is littered with signs of meaningless confusion associated with different aspects of human activity: signs of combat show no ending, neither corpses nor footsteps leading away; torture implements, evidences of human villainy, rust away; agricultural leavings rot by villainous chance. The pattern of emptiness forces [Roland] in the end to accept lack of meaning and admit defeat in his search for pattern.

Is this, in fact, if we accept Cadbury's reading, a moment in the poem which anticipates the loss, among Browning's contemporaries, of those certainties, social, political or religious, taken for granted among earlier generations? It is then that the hero "realizes that there is no moral value in the world for him to find". The tower, according to Cadbury, "becomes the quintessence of the disorder with which he had been faced before, but which he had refused to admit". Roland now has something to fight, "and the discovery of the lack of order is in itself an ordering".

But are the symbolic elements in fact Roland's own inventions? E. Warwick Slinn, in *Browning And*

The Fictions Of Identity, maintains that if the hero is the victim of fate, it is his own consciousness which makes this appear so. The so-called evil and decay within the landscape are qualities we have to take on trust, a kind of rationale imposed on the whole scene by Roland's attempt to make sense of it. "His use of similes makes it clear that most of the images which characterise his journey are the result of Roland's own speculations." His inner projections assemble the sinister and eerie panorama which unfurls before the reader. Leprosy, serpents, the devil's hoof, water-rats, toads, wild cats and boils are all products of the wandering knight's fevered imagination. The overwhelming solitariness of his adventure drives him back into the recesses of his inner world. "As the supports of social convention are stripped away and nature," according to Slinn's reading of the poem, "is found to be barren, inhospitable and indifferent, unable to act for itself, all comes to focus on Roland himself and his own resources."

Ultimately, in this interpretation, *Childe Roland* dramatises "the paradox of meaningful action in a meaningless wasteland", in which any significance is provided by the lone protagonist's unaided decoding of its symbolic language as he conceives it to exist. Those who prefer to read Browning within a strictly 19th-century context may choose to see this process of decipherment as reflecting the pointlessness of romantic heroism in a prosaic, over-mechanised and essentially hideous world created by Victorian capitalism and industrialisation. So is *Childe Roland* perhaps a veiled protest against the same sort of spiritual wilderness being attacked by Charles Dickens? He was writing his novel *Hard Times*, an assault on the unrelenting grimness of life in northern factory towns, at the same time as Browning was working on *Men And Women*, which included our poem.

This approach is given further emphasis by John Woolford and Daniel Karlin in an important study of various aspects of Browning's achievement, published in 1996. They see *Childe Roland To The Dark Tower Came* as "expressing a sense of having failed in a socio-political mission to involve poetry in contemporary society". The poet's choice of a knightly romance as the vehicle for this sense of failure ironically reflects the Victorian idea that this is exactly the kind of story poets should be handling, as in the case of Alfred Tennyson's Arthurian sequence *Idylls Of The King*. These, most of which appeared after Browning's poem was written, were designed to mirror the preoccupations of mid-Victorian Britain, more especially in their emphasis on the values of truth, loyalty, sincerity and faith in the broadest sense of the term. By upholding these, the Arthurian knights of the *Idylls* can successfully engage with the task of holding back a tide of evil threatening to engulf the world.

Childe Roland, on the other hand, is "defecting from his quest" by pursuing his potentially suicidal mission to reach the Dark Tower. "His abandonment of solidarity with the other questors inverts into solidarity with those who have failed before him," according to Woolford and Karlin – though there is in fact no indication in the relevant stanzas XVI and XVII that Roland endorses the behaviour which has caused his former comrades' downfall. In this reading of the poem "the unintelligibility of the landscape, of its origin and of its apotheosis, the Dark Tower, combine into a critique of the quest itself as a meaning-giving action".

Such an interpretation, implicitly rejecting the loftier purposes of works like *Idylls Of The King* and making *Childe Roland* into an "anti-quest" poem, accords with the view of it advanced by earlier Browning critics such as Harold Bloom and Betty Miller. These critics see the work as embodying the writer's awareness of his own failure to advance his specific goals as a poet and of his distinct inferiority to the Romantic poets of the previous generation, more especially his beloved Shelley. The awful possibility at the close of *Childe Roland* is that there may actually be nothing inside the Dark Tower. The enemy is no longer an armed and mounted knight, ready to inflict physical harm on his assailant, but something more terrifying for its incorporeal, abstract nature, a force or a power represented by elements such as money, hierarchy, social influence, political and religious ideologies or the complexities revealed by scientific research – the invisible but nevertheless palpable fears, in short, of our modern age.

Miller and Bloom offer still more compelling views of the poem as having close links with Browning's psychological trauma in suppressing his earliest, Shelley-influenced poetic manner "as a sacrifice to his Oedipal anxieties, to his love for his Evangelical mother". Bloom compares *Childe Roland* to the great poems of Samuel Taylor Coleridge, *Christabel, The Rime Of The Ancient Mariner* and *Kubla Khan*, calling it "a ballad of the imagination's revenge against the poet's unpoetic nature", praising its "terrible opening to vision" and "the extraordinary negative intensity of Childe Roland's consciousness". The hero is depicted by the critic as "marching into that land of his own terrible force of failed will". The knights who stumbled in their quest are interpreted by Bloom as Browning's Romantic precursors, "failing triumphantly". Revelation may not rescue Roland/Browning but it allows him to "die in the courage of knowing".

Finally, what had Browning himself to tell his readers as regarded the conundrum of *Childe Roland To The Dark Tower Came*? Poets are often deliberately unhelpful when asked to "explain" their works or furnish definitive meanings for them. The whole point of poetry is, after all that it doesn't supply a system of correspondences and explanations to the reader; reading a poem is an act of imaginative collaboration between us and the writer and it is absurdly reductive to expect a work like *Childe Roland* to be accompanied by a set of footnotes identifying the precise significance of its extraordinary range of symbols and images. Browning never went so far as to link any of the elements here with specific areas of meaning. When, towards the end of his life, somebody suggested allegorical equivalents for them, he backed away from this solution. "Oh no, not at all," he declared.

> Understand, I don't repudiate either. I only mean I was conscious of no allegorical intention in writing it. *Childe Roland* came upon me as a kind of dream. I had to write it then and there, and I finished it in the same day, I believe. But it was simply that I had to do it. I did not know then what I meant beyond that, and I'm sure I don't know now. But I am very fond of it.

The dreamscape holds its secret and our fascination endures.

Why do we love *My Last Duchess?*

My Last Duchess is one of Browning's most popular and frequently anthologised poems. For many of the poet's admirers it sums up his uncanny ability to make his readers love the unworthiest of human beings by simply enabling such characters to reveal their innermost selves through the medium of the dramatic monologue. Certain among the cast of *The Ring And The Book* illustrate this perfectly, as do figures such as Andrea Del Sarto, Bishop Blougram or his Renaissance avatar who orders such a handsome tomb at Saint Praxed's church. These people are often what the Victorians liked to term "cads" or "bounders", individuals who, like the would-be opera diva in *Youth And Art*, are "no better than they should be". They are not by any means outcasts from their society, but they certainly don't deserve the social and material advantages they seem to have been given in such abundance.

There are obvious exceptions to this pattern. *Fra Lippo Lippi* is a case in point. We ought to think the errant friar, caught chasing whores down a Florentine back alley, a thoroughly unworthy creature, yet he emerges as an admirable incarnation of that archetypally modern ideal, the artist who lives purely for his vocation and has little or no regard for the conventions and taboos governing the lives of others (more especially those of his fellow monks). The youthful David, the speaker in *Saul*, is another instance of the poet's absorption with the power of creative spirits to shape the lives of those around them. Nowadays we might well find the mentally disturbed figure of Biblical Israel's first king more arresting than that of the boy harpist whose music offered him a therapy for his depression, and who as an adult would eventually take over his kingdom. Browning enables us, nevertheless, to share in David's wonder at the divine potency of his own musical gifts, so that *Saul* appears less of a straightforward dramatic monologue than a hymn in praise of music and, we can safely infer, of its extraordinary grip on the imagination of the poet himself.

In the case of *My Last Duchess*, on the other hand, we are dealing with a man who, if not himself a murderer, may have been responsible for ordering

A MODERN "LAST DUCHESS'?

The sources for Browning's poems are often a fascinating mixture of the well-known, the not-so-familiar and the amazingly obscure. It is quite possible that the poet, in creating his Duke in *My Last Duchess*, may have heard a story connected with the Tuscan aristocrat and liberal politician Baron Bettino Ricasoli (1809-1890). As a young man he married, following approved custom, a woman of his own class, the daughter of a Florentine nobleman. One winter evening the pair attended a ball at one of the city's grandest palaces. It was permissible, on such occasions, for wives to dance with other men besides their husbands, but Ricasoli grew suspicious of the attentions being paid to his pretty young Baroness by a certain nobleman in the ballroom. When these two had finished their waltz, she found herself swept away by her husband the death of his wife and who clearly feels that the business of ensuring that "all smiles stopped together" is an entirely natural requirement of somebody in his particular rank of society. The role of the listener here is more important than usual in Browning's poems. So often such characters are simply there to be spoken to – or spoken at. Here the ambassador accompanying the Duke through his picture gallery is someone we stop to think about, for he will have a number of highly significant issues on which to ponder at the close of the poem.

---

with the words "We are leaving now". The Ricasoli carriage was called, but when the coachman, surprised at their quitting the ball so early, asked whether he should take them home, Ricasoli gave orders instead that they were to be driven to the family castle at Broglio, about 20 miles' distance from the city.

The Baroness was wearing only a ballgown and a silk shawl, it was a cold night and snow had started to fall. The coachman drove off as bidden, and they arrived at Broglio in the small hours of the morning. Beds were prepared for them in the castle, but Ricasoli made no attempt to explain his behaviour to his wife. The next morning he announced that he would be leaving for Florence. "You, however, will remain here," he told her. And there indeed, for the rest of her long life, Baroness Ricasoli stayed. Her husband visited several times a year, the pair had children, but she was never allowed back to her native city. And all because he was jealous of the way she had smiled at another man. From this story, with a proud and inflexible aristocrat at its centre, Browning may have taken the hint for the character of his haughty Duke of Ferrara in *My Last Duchess* ∎

Browning published *My Last Duchess* in 1842, as part of a privately-printed pamphlet entitled "Dramatic Lyrics". The scene is the north Italian city of Ferrara, famous during the Renaissance as the capital of a duchy ruled by the art-loving Estense family. The last Estense duke was Alfonso II (1558-1597), described by a contemporary as "a man [whose] strong character and remarkable abilities, handsome person, dignified presence and gallant bearing endeared him to his people". Alfonso patronised poets, artists and musicians, following the tradition of his forebears, and surrounded Ferrara itself with a series of delightful parks and gardens.

Unhappiness clouded his personal life. His three marriages brought him no children and it was rumoured that his first wife, the Florentine princess Lucrezia de' Medici, had been poisoned for her infidelity only three years after their wedding. Her successor Barbara von Habsburg, daughter of the Count of the Tyrol, lasted little longer, and the third duchess, Margherita Gonzaga of Mantua, was a frivolous creature who preferred hunting and parties to playing the role of a dignified ducal consort. With Alfonso's death the duchy of Ferrara was seized by the Pope, and the city, which Browning first visited some years after composing *My Last Duchess*, became a sleepy market town living on its recollections of former greatness.

Out of this moment in late Renaissance Italian history the poet worked up one of his most striking and fearsome characters. For though we learn a lot about the Duchess – she and her fate were plainly suggested by Lucrezia de' Medici – we develop an uncomfortably close acquaintance with her husband. The very first line of the poem

That's my last Duchess painted on the wall

induces a shiver for its casual style. How many others have there been, the ambassador may well wonder, and, as the Italians themselves say: "What end did they make?" The Duke's subsequent words, "I call that piece a wonder now", imply an important distinction in his mind between the Duchess as a human being and the presentation of her as a work of art. His attitude to her in either capacity is proprietorial, as if by right. He owns his wife as both a woman and a picture, and the source of his initial outrage is that she should have dared to smile at anybody other than her husband. He cannot – more importantly, he will not – tolerate the generosity with which she bestows the privilege of her smile.

> *...Her looks went everywhere.*
> *Sir, 'twas all one! My favour at her breast,*
> *The dropping of the daylight in the West,*
> *The bough of cherries some officious fool*
> *Broke in the orchard for her.*

He cannot bear the notion that

> *...she ranked*
> *My gift of a nine-hundred-years-old name*
> *With anybody's gift*

But he is far too arrogant to express his irritation openly to her. Browning, at this stage of his career, was not especially keen to cultivate friendships among the aristocracy, and though later on he became a welcome figure at dinners and evening parties given by titled families living in London, he was never noted as being particularly snobbish or eager to hobnob with lords and ladies. That uncanny intuition typical of a gifted writer enabled him to grasp one of the crucial features of an aristocratic mindset, namely that it distrusts displays of emotion and, more particularly, the business of talking about emotion.

How much was Browning influenced by his wife?

Robert Browning's marriage to Elizabeth Barrett was the most important event in his life. Her presence, whether as a wife or as a fellow poet – her literary reputation was already confirmed by the time his first poems were published – had a major impact on his mature work. This influence was crucial, both on his artistic development and on the way in which he viewed his poetic vocation within the wider context of the Victorian cultural scene. The beginnings of their relationship, however, were unusual. They did not meet until after at least a year of exchanging letters with one another, and both poets were hardly in the first flush of youth. Browning was 36, Elizabeth 41, but the love affair which began in earnest with their first meeting, on 20 May 1845, had to be carried on in absolute secrecy.

This clandestine courtship has always lent a bloom of sentimental intrigue to what might otherwise have been a perfectly orthodox wooing. The unusual conditions were imposed by the brooding presence of Elizabeth's father, Edward Moulton Barrett. A domestic tyrant even by Victorian standards, he had formerly owned slaves in Jamaica, and the inevitable connection has been made between this fact and his extraordinary domination over a household of 12 adult children, none of whom was allowed to receive suitors or wed without his approval, unlikely as this was. One of Elizabeth's brothers would later be disinherited for marrying without permission and her two sisters had endured the seeing-off of several young admirers. In the spirit of what one Browning biographer has called Mr Barrett's "strange pseudo-religious tyranny", there was no likelihood that he would ever let Elizabeth, his eldest daughter and favourite child, lead an independent existence as a wife and mother – though, ironically, she herself had inherited much of this possessiveness in her attitude towards her siblings.

In their life of Browning, *The Book, The Ring And The Poet* (1974), William Irvine and Park Honan claim that "his exploit was his own romance", calling the secret love affair with Elizabeth

> the daring rescue of a pessimist by an optimist... a stratagem against an ogre, the awakening of a sleeping princess in an enchanted palace... the wooing of a confirmed old maid by a confirmed bachelor, an Orphic descent into a region of shadows and the guiding of an Eurydice upward into the light.

The whole liaison was further complicated, in its earliest stages, by Elizabeth's status as a sofa-bound invalid, suffering from a lingering tubercular illness and the effects of spinal injury from a riding accident. Things were made no easier by her increased sense of family duty following the deaths of her mother, worn out by serial pregnancy, and of a favourite brother, drowned while sailing in Cornwall.

Under the benign influence of her growing attachment to Browning, however, she began to recover her physical strength, but the shadow of Mr Barrett and his suspicions hung over every meeting between the pair. Robert was allowed to visit the house at 50 Wimpole Street, in his capacity as a

Opposite: Elizabeth Barrett Browning

literary man and an admirer of Elizabeth's work, but only the two Barrett sisters, Henrietta and Arabel, had any inkling of what had happened or – more dangerously – of what was about to happen.

The London summer of 1846 was the hottest hitherto recorded and the metropolis, with its inadequate sanitation and street-cleaning, became decidedly unhealthy. Mr Barrett's plan to move the family to a rented house in Surrey was the signal for Robert and Elizabeth to act decisively, and on 11 September the pair were married at Marylebone parish church, with Elizabeth's maid acting as witness. A week later, via a series of elaborate subterfuges, they left for the Continent, settling first in Pisa and then in Florence, the city which became their permanent home. Before leaving, Elizabeth wrote letters to her father and her brother George. After five years the latter forgave her. Mr Barrett cast his daughter off altogether, disinheriting her and rejecting any attempt at reconciliation.

The elopement of these two mature adults seemed scandalous to many. Elizabeth incurred censure as an undutiful daughter, prepared to bring shame on her family by disobeying her father, and she always felt guilty for having betrayed his trust.

But in the Victorian era, whatever their scruples as to duty and morality, many people came to see the marriage of these two poets as a perfect union between two super-fine creative spirits, sanctified still further by the fact that several other writers of

Bill Travers, John Gielgud & Jennifer Jones as Robert Browning, Edward Moulton-Barrett & Elizabeth Barrett in The Barretts of Wimpole Street

the period – Charles Dickens and Thomas Hardy among them – had such an unhappy experience of wedlock. But just how durable and satisfying a marital relationship was Robert and Elizabeth's?

Despite attempts by some Browning biographers, notably Betty Miller in her 1952 portrait, to suggest that the marriage was a failure, evidence suggests that the pair were happy and fulfilled as husband and wife. There were, admittedly, some major disagreements. One was over spiritualism, a fashionable new craze towards which Elizabeth was drawn but he remained sceptical. Another was over the merits of the French emperor Napoleon III, whom Browning considered a disreputable fake but

Elizabeth worshipped as the man who would help her beloved Italians to become a unified nation at last. They had their differences, too, on the subject of bringing up their only child, Robert Wiedemann Browning, known as "Pennini" or "Pen" for short. Hopelessly spoilt by his mother and dressed in ridiculously girlish outfits when a little boy, he grew up to be conspicuously unremarkable, contriving to marry a rich American heiress and living off her fortune in a Venetian palace.

For the most part, though, the Brownings dwelt contentedly together in Florence, Rome and Paris, with occasional trips to London, where Elizabeth managed to mend one or two fences with her siblings, if not with her perpetually wounded father. She was a shrewd and painstaking critic of Browning's poetry and while she was alive her own literary success, especially with the verse novel *Aurora Leigh* (1856), was often greater than his. Robert dedicated his *Men And Women* to her, and certain of his poems, especially *By The Fireside,* are directly inspired by the sense of liberation which their marriage gave him. Elizabeth tried patiently to point her husband towards a greater clarity of expression, encouraging him to smooth over certain rough edges of diction and metrical experiment – though some readers have wished that she had been more successful in this respect.

Ultimately this happy partnership was doomed by Elizabeth's increasing physical weakness, not helped by the exhausting emotional intensity with which she had always tended to involve herself in any issue which interested her. The struggle for Italian unity and independence from Austrian domination had engaged her from the moment she and Browning moved to Florence in 1847. She watched with dismay the failure of nationwide revolutions the following year, but was more optimistic when, a decade later, it seemed as if her adored Emperor Napoleon III would lead his French army to victory in Italy, drive out the Austrians and unite the Italians at last. When Britain's Tory government refused to get involved and the Emperor, having defeated the Austrians in Lombardy, failed to complete his mission, signing a peace treaty instead, she was devastated. News of her sister Henrietta's death from cancer shattered her completely and she told a friend that "I struggle to live on". Her own dormant illness now took a serious hold and she died on 28 June 1861 at their Florence house, Casa Guidi. Her last words to Browning were "My Robert! – my heavens, my beloved! Our lives are held by God!"

Though other women would later give him affection, care and inspiration, figures such as his sister Sarianna, his friends Isa Blagden, Julia Wedgwood or Katherine Bronson, none of these could ever replicate Elizabeth Barrett's extraordinary impact on Robert Browning. Whatever the complexities of their relationship, its value in terms of his development as a poet was immeasurable. *Men And Women*, representing his finest literary achievement, is its direct result and Elizabeth's encouragement was critical in strengthening a sense of his own vocation. Given how little of his later poetry is nowadays enjoyed by the general reader, we are free to consider how different his work would have been during the 1860s and 1870s if Elizabeth had survived to influence him.

Why read Browning?

Robert Browning was one of the most influential 19th-century poets. His impact can be felt on the work of poets as distinct from one another in their individual voices as Thomas Hardy, T.S. Eliot and Robert Frost. We can trace another direct line of descent, through Ezra Pound, who acknowledged Browning's central influence on him, to many of the major figures in 20th-century American poetry. The great Browning critic Robert Langbaum sees the poet's mastery of the dramatic monologue as a crucial inspiration for the work of W.B. Yeats and Robert Lowell, identifying him as an essential forerunner of modernism, whose "innovations are part of a general change of sensibility – a demand that all literature yield much the same effect, an effect of lyrical intensity". Later in the same essay, "The Dramatic Monologue: Sympathy Versus Judgment" (1957), Langbaum shows how the monologue becomes "an appropriate form for an empiricist and relativist age, an age which has come to consider value as an evolving thing dependent upon the changing individual and social requirements of the historical process".

Yet for all his looming presence on the 19th-century poetic scene and the long shadow it casts over British and American poets during the hundred years following his death, Browning is still a writer who provokes question and controversy. How successful was he during his own lifetime? Several moments in his career forced him to confront outright failure. His attempts at establishing himself as a dramatist during the 1840s were doomed to disaster and the only one of his eight plays nowadays read (and, very occasionally, acted) is *Pippa Passes*, a masterpiece for reasons which have more to do with its powerfully-imagined storyline than with any real genius for theatre on the writer's part.

Certain of the longer poems provide notorious examples of Browning's obsessively mannered diction and sheer, intractable obscurity of expression, baffling or simply infuriating to the reader. *Sordello* , for example, on whose publication in 1840 the poet staked so much in terms of his reputation, was generally considered incomprehensible from start to finish. Tennyson famously remarked that the only two lines of it he understood were the first

Who will, may hear Sordello's story told

and the last

Who would, has heard Sordello's story told

and that each of them was a lie. Two substantial later poems, *Prince Hohenstiel Schwangau*, a satire on the recently deposed French emperor Napoleon III, and *Balaustion's Adventure*, a Greek woman's account of witnessing the first performance of the *Alcestis* of Euripides, are other casualties of a tendency among the poet's readers to give up at the first signs of difficulty, though each is well worth the effort involved in tackling it.

Perhaps we would be wiser to accept G.K. Chesterton's assessment of the supposedly obscure Browning as "an intellectual democrat", a writer who quite innocently assumed that his readers were as erudite and eclectic in their culture as he was, and who paid them the compliment of expecting them to rise to his level rather than taking their ignorance for granted. As George Eliot, typically fair-minded, says, "in his best poems he makes us feel that what we took for obscurity in him was superficiality in ourselves". A poet for the faint-hearted he certainly isn't, but by the same token he encourages us not to be mentally idle, stimulates our curiosity and uses his own quite astounding breadth of knowledge both to challenge and to entertain his readers.

However Browningesque other poets may appear, there is nobody else in world poetry quite like

Browning himself. Only Shakespeare and Chaucer rival him in that quality which, for want of a better word, we call "universality", the gift of being able to enter into multiple states of being and register human experience with an unnerving accuracy and authenticity. He mirrors the preoccupations and concerns of his own age, but is not so narrowly Victorian that he cannot transcend its prejudices, taboos and petty anxieties. His vision of life involves a deeply compassionate comprehensiveness. Figures such as Andrea del Sarto, Bishop Blougram, the unscrupulous spiritualist medium Mr Sludge or, indeed, most of the main characters in *The Ring And The Book,* are made memorable for us because of the way in which Browning, aware of their vices, follies or personal inadequacies, seems to argue so eloquently on their behalf in his capacity as a fellow human being. Their frankness with us – in ironic contrast, some might say, with Browning's own reticence regarding himself – invites some sort of admiration, however grudging. In this way they justify themselves to both God and the world, despite their failings and misdeeds.

For those who fall under his spell as a poet, Browning needs no such self-justification. The versatility which produced poems as different from one another in mood, form and style as *Meeting At Night, The Last Ride Together, The Pied Piper Of Hamelin* and *My Last Duchess* was matched by a genuine integrity and singlemindedness in their creator's engagement with his artistic vocation. In his last collection, *Asolando*, Browning wrote a final testament for himself in a poem entitled *Epilogue*. Some lines of its second and third stanzas bring us as close as we shall ever come to the writer's idea of who he actually was and what he believed in:

> *What had I on earth to do*
> *With the slothful, with the mawkish, the unmanly?*
> *Like the aimless, helpless, hopeless, did I drivel?*
> *– Being – who?*
> *One who never turned his back but marched*
> *breast forward,*
> *Never doubted clouds would break,*
> *Never dreamed, though rights were*
> *worsted, wrong would triumph,*
> *Held we fall to rise, are baffled to fight better,*
> *Sleep to wake.*

A few days before he died, Browning read the poem to his sister and daughter-in-law, then declared: "It almost sounds like bragging to say this, and as if I ought to cancel it; but it's the simple truth; and as it's true, it shall stand."

BROWNING ON HIS OWN POETRY...

"You do what I always wanted, hoped to do, and only seem now likely to do for the first time. You speak out, you – I only make men & women speak – give you truth broken into prismatic hues, & fear the pure white light, even if it is in me: but I am going to try..."
From a letter to Elizabeth Barrett, 13 January 1845

"I know that I don't make out my conception by my language; all poetry being a putting the infinite within the finite."
From a letter to John Ruskin, 10 December 1855.

"I never designed to puzzle people, as some of my critics have supposed. On the other hand, I never pretended to offer such literature as should be a substitute for a cigar or a game of dominoes to an idle man."
From a letter to Thomas Carlyle about *Men And Women*, 1855.

...AND TWO ANONYMOUS REVIEWS

"His mode of thought, without being anti-English, constantly bears an indescribable savour of the Continent."
Quarterly Review, 1860.

"It is really high time that this sort of thing should, if possible, be stopped. Here is another book of madness and mysticism."
Saturday Review, 1854, on *Men And Women*.

FOUR CONTEMPORARY VIEWS

"*He does not take possession of our souls and set them aglow, as the greatest poets, the greatest artists do. We admire his power, we are not subdued by it. Language with him does not seem spontaneously to link itself into song, as sounds link themselves into melody in the mind of the creative musician; he rather seems by his commanding powers to compel language into verse.*"
George Eliot, 1856.

"*This is my Elixir of Life!*"
Dante Gabriel Rossetti, 1856, on *Men And Women*.

"*Browning has got a way of talking (and making his people talk) with the air and spirit of a man bouncing up from table with his mouth full of bread and cheese and saying that he meant to stand no blasted nonsense.*"
Gerard Manley Hopkins, 1881.

"*Yes, Browning was great. And as what will he be remembered? As a poet? Ah, not as a poet! He will be remembered as a writer of fiction, as the most supreme writer of fiction, it may be, that we have ever had... He used poetry as a medium for writing prose.*"
Oscar Wilde, 1890.

A SHORT CHRONOLOGY

1812 Robert Browning born on 7th May at Camberwell, south-east London, only son of Robert Browning, scholar, book-lover and bank-clerk, and his wife Sarah Anna Wiedemann.

1814 Browning's sister Sarianna born.

1820-26 Browning attends Thomas Ready's school in Peckham.

1828 Browning spends a year studying at the newly-founded London University.

1833 His first major poem, *Pauline*, is published.

1834 Browning visits St Petersburg.

1838 His first visit to Italy, centred on Venice and the neighbouring town of Asolo.

1841 Browning begins to publish poems and plays in a series of volumes entitled *Bells And Pomegranates*.

1844 He makes a second visit to Italy, this time to Naples, Rome and Florence.

1845 Browning writes his first letter to Elizabeth Barrett and is soon visiting her family's town house in Wimpole Street, London.

1846 By now in love, Robert and Elizabeth plan to elope. They marry on 12th September and leave England for Pisa, Italy.

1847 They move to Florence, settling at Casa Guidi.

1849 Their son Robert Wiedemann Browning, known as "Pen", is born.

1855 *Men And Women*, Browning's most successful poetic collection, is published.

1861 Elizabeth dies and is buried in Florence. Browning returns to London.

1863 His three-volume *Poetical Works* is published.

1864 Publication of *Dramatis Personae*. Browning begins *The Ring And The Book*, a narrative based on a 17th-century Italian trial record he purchased in Rome four years earlier.

1868 *The Ring And The Book* is published.

1878 Browning renews his acquaintance with Italy.

1881 The Browning Society is founded in London by admirers of the poet's work. Similar societies are soon founded all over the world.

1887 Pen Browning marries the American heiress Fannie Coddington and the pair settle in Venice, where Browning himself soon joins them.

1889 On 12th December *Asolando*, Browning's last book of verse, is published. He dies in Venice later that day and is buried in Poets' Corner, Westminster Abbey

BIBLIOGRAPHY

Altick, Richard D, and James F. Loucks, *Browning's Roman Murder Story*, University of Chicago Press, 1968Armstrong, Isobel, *Victorian Poetry, Poetics and Politics,* Routledge, 1993

Bloom, Harold, *The Ringers in the Tower: Studies in Romantic Tradition*, University of Chicago Press, 1971

Browning, Robert, *The Poems*, 2 vols, edited by John Pettigrew and Thomas J. Collins Penguin, 1981

Chesterton, G.K., *Robert Browning*, Macmillan, 1906

George Eliot, Review of "Men and Women", *The Westminster Review*, 1856

Finlayson, Iain, *Browning*, Harper Collins 2004

Gibson, Mary Ellis, Critical Essays on Robert Browning G. K. Hall 1992

Hawlin, Stefan, *The Complete Critical Guide to Robert Browning,* Routledge, 2001

Ingersoll, E.G., Lacan, Browning and the Murderous Voyeur, *Victorian Poetry 28*, 1990

James, Henry, *Browning in Westminster Abbey*, Houghton Mifflin, 1905

Karlin, Daniel, *The Courtship of Robert Browning and Elizabeth Barret*, OUP, 1985

Karlin, Daniel, *Browning's Hatreds*, OUP, 1993

Kennedy, *Richard S, Robert Browning's 'Asolando': The Indian Summer of A Poe*t, University of Missouri Press, 1993

Korg, Jacob, *Browning and Italy*, Ohio University Press, 1983

Langbaum, Robert, *The Poetry of Experience: the Dramatic Monologue in Literary Tradition*, University of Chicago Press, 1957

Litzinger, Boyd, and Harold Leslie Knickerbocker, *The Browning Critics,* University of Kentucky Press, 1965

Roberts, Adam ed., *Robert Browning*, OUP, 1997

Slinn, E.Warwick, *Browning and the Fictions of Identity*, Macmillan, 1982

Thomas, Donald S, *Robert Browning: A Life within Life*, Viking, 1982

Woolford, John ed, *Robert Browning in Contexts*, Wedgestone, 1998

INDEX

First published in 2012 by
Connell Guides

Spye Arch House
Spye Park
Lacock
Chippenham
Wiltshire SN15 2PR

10 9 8 7 6 5 4 3 2 1

Picture credits:

p.11 © Look and Learn/ Bridgeman Art Library
p.15 © National Portrait Gallery
p.31 © World History Archive/ Alamy
p.41 © Corbis
p.47 © Harrogate Museums and Arts/ The Bridgeman Art Library
p.53 © Alamy
p.71 © Lebrecht Authors
p.85 © The Maas Gallery, London / Bridgeman Art Library
p.93 © The Higgins Art Gallery & Museum, Bedford, UK / Bridgeman Art Library
p.109 © Classic Image/ Alamy
p.111 © Alamy

A CIP catalogue record for this book is available from the British Library.

ISBN 978-1-907776-11-3

Design © Nathan Burton
Assistant editor: Katie Sanderson
Printed in Great Britain by Butler Tanner & Dennis

www.connellguides.com